Guidebook to Better English
Level 4

Phoenix Learning Resources

NEW YORK

TO THE STUDENT

The purpose of *Guidebook to Better English* is to help you improve your language skills. The ability to listen, speak, and write effectively is an important part of communication. Careful study of this guidebook will help you to understand and use the English language.

The guidebook has all the information you need to complete the lessons. It is divided in the following way:

- eighty-one lessons, separated into nine units of nine lessons, with a review at the end of each unit; followed by
- *Guides*, containing rules, explanations, examples, practice exercises, and answers to the practice exercises; followed by
- *Answers to Exercises*, containing the answers for the lessons in each unit; followed by
- *Index to Guides*; followed by
- *Score Chart* for recording your scores.

A test will be given after you finish each unit. The tests are in a separate book.

Read the following steps before beginning your work in the guidebook:

- Turn to the first lesson. Notice the symbol under the title of the lesson. The symbol points to the numbered guide or guides most important to the lesson.
- Turn to *Guides* and find the numbers of the guides pointed out by the symbol. Study the guides and the examples. Then do the practice exercises. Check your answers with those given in the answer box. Study the guides again. Correct any mistakes you may have made.
- Turn back to the lesson page. Read the directions and any examples that are given. Then finish the lesson.
- Turn to *Answers to Exercises*. Check your answers with those given in that section.
- Record your score at the top of the lesson page. Then record it on the chart on the inside back cover of this book.
- Study the guides again. Correct any mistakes you may have made.

In each unit of this guidebook, you will find two other activities: WORDSEARCH and COMPOSITION. WORDSEARCH helps build your vocabulary. It can also improve your listening and speaking habits. COMPOSITION shows you how to use the skills of a unit in a written form.

The language skills that you learn can become a part of your speaking and writing. After you have finished the course, you may use this guidebook whenever you need information about language.

Copyright © 1989, 1982 by Phoenix Learning Resources, Inc. All Rights Reserved.
No part of this publication may be reproduced, stored in a retrieval system, or transmitted, in any form or by any means, electronic, mechanical, photocopying, recording, or otherwise, without the prior written permission of the publisher.
Printed in the United States of America.

ISBN 0-7915-1265-7

(previously ISBN 0-07-374258-9)

3 4 5 6 7 8 9 0   99 98 97 96 95 94 93

CONTENTS

Lesson   **UNIT I**

1. Recognizing Sentences 5
2. Identifying Kinds of Sentences 6
3. Recognizing Subjects, Verbs, and Direct Objects 7
4. Writing Subjective Complements 8
5. Recognizing Subjective Complements 9
6. Using Natural Word Order 10
7. Choosing Appropriate Forms 11
8. Capitalizing 12
9. Punctuating 13
10. Review I 14

UNIT II

11. Recognizing Simple and Compound Sentences 15
12. Writing Compound Sentences 16
13. Using Compound Elements 17
14. Combining Sentences 18
15. Punctuating Sentences 19
16. Forming Plurals and Possessives 20
17. Using Nouns as Indirect Objects 21
18. Recognizing Nouns 22
19. Using Capitalization and Punctuation 23
20. Review II 24

UNIT III

21. Identifying Prepositions and Prepositional Phrases 25
22. Identifying Nouns and Pronouns 26
23. Identifying Kinds of Pronouns 27
24. Identifying Kinds of Pronouns 28
25. Recognizing Pronouns as Sentence Elements 29
26. Learning about Pronoun Agreement 30
27. Using Pronouns 31
28. Using a Dictionary to Find Information 32
29. Choosing Appropriate Forms 33
30. Review III 34

UNIT IV

31. Identifying Adjectives 35
32. Recognizing Predicate Adjectives 36
33. Combining Sentences 37
34. Recognizing Adverbs 38
35. Identifying Adverbs 39
36. Recognizing Prepositional Phrases 40
37. Identifying Prepositional Phrases 41
38. Correcting a Paragraph 42
39. Using Capitalization and Punctuation 43
40. Review IV 44

UNIT V

41. Writing Verb Forms 45

Lesson   **UNIT V**

42. Recognizing Subject-Verb Agreement 46
43. Choosing Subject-Verb Agreement 47
44. Using Verbs 48
45. Recognizing Verb Tenses 49
46. Using Active and Passive Voice 50
47. Forming Contractions 51
48. Choosing Appropriate Forms 52
49. Using Capitalization and Punctuation 53
50. Review V 54

UNIT VI

51. Recognizing Verbals—Participles 55
52. Using Participial Phrases 56
53. Recognizing Verbals—Gerunds 57
54. Using Gerund Phrases 58
55. Recognizing Verbals—Infinitives 59
56. Using Infinitive Phrases 60
57. Choosing Synonyms and Antonyms 61
58. Using Appropriate Forms 62
59. Writing a Paragraph 63
60. Review VI 64

UNIT VII

61. Recognizing Dependent Clauses 65
62. Writing Complex Sentences 66
63. Writing Complex Sentences 67
64. Recognizing Adjective Clauses 68
65. Recognizing Adverb Clauses 69
66. Combining Sentences 70
67. Choosing Appropriate Forms 71
68. Revising a Paragraph 72
69. Writing a Paragraph 73
70. Review VII 74

UNIT VIII

71. Writing a Business Letter 75
72. Writing a Business Letter 76
73. Writing a Business Letter 77
74. Completing an Application Form 78
75. Completing an Employment Test 79
76. Finding Information 80
77. Writing a Paragraph 81
78. Choosing Appropriate Forms 82
79. Using a Dictionary—Word Division 83
80. Review VIII 84

UNIT IX

81. Reviewing Sentences 85
82. Reviewing Sentence Elements 86
83. Reviewing Verbals 87
84. Reviewing Dependent Clauses 88
85. Reviewing Verbs and Adverbs 89
86. Reviewing Compound Elements 90
87. Reviewing Parts of Speech 91

Lesson **UNIT IX**

- *88* Reviewing Appropriate Forms 92
- *89* Reviewing Capitalization and Punctuation 93
- *90* Review IX 94–96

Guides 97
Answers to Exercises 146
Index to Guides 160

Name _____ Perfect Score 37 My Score _____

UNIT I/*LESSON 1*

Recognizing Sentences

▷ GUIDES *1a, b, 2a, b*

Part I: Punctuate each group of words that is a sentence. Mark an X after each group of words that is not a sentence. (Score: 12)

1. The 1980 Winter Olympic Games
2. Lake Placid, New York, hosted the games
3. The United States' Olympic team won ten gold medals
4. The Russians won nine gold medals
5. Didn't the U.S. hockey team beat the Russian team
6. Yes, in one of the most exciting events of the games
7. Eric Heiden of the U.S. won all five men's speed-skating events
8. Set records in each event
9. Did his sister Beth win any medals
10. A bronze medal in the women's 3,000-meter speed-skating
11. Have you tried bobsledding
12. The bobsled and luge races are my favorite events

Part II: Write four sentences about the Olympic Games and the events you like best. (Score: 20—5 for each sentence)

13. _____

14. _____

15. _____

16. _____

▷ GUIDE *59 WORDSEARCH* (Score: 5) _____

1. diagnosis   prescription   surgery   recovery
2. law   chemistry   medicine

Discussion: Include the words in row 1 as you discuss the importance of the profession named in WORDSEARCH.

Name _____   Perfect Score 42   My Score _____

UNIT I/LESSON 2

Identifying Kinds of Sentences

▷ GUIDE 2a–d

Part I: Punctuate each sentence. On the line write the abbreviation that tells whether the sentence is declarative, interrogative, exclamatory, or imperative. Use these abbreviations: *declar., interrog., exclam., imper.* (Score: 22—2 for each sentence)

1. Have you heard of Famous Amos _____

2. He's famous for his chocolate chip cookies _____

3. How good a crunchy cookie would taste right now _____

4. Please stop talking about food _____

5. Wasn't Wally Amos once a successful talent agent _____

6. Yes, but then he fell on hard times _____

7. What could he do to earn a living _____

8. What a great idea he had _____

9. Wasn't he inspired by his Aunt Della's recipe _____

10. Now Famous Amos bakes over three tons of cookies a day _____

11. One of his cookie studios is in Nutley, N.J., isn't it _____

Part II: Write a declarative, an interrogative, an exclamatory, and an imperative sentence about a food product you enjoy or about a place where you like to eat. (Score: 20—5 for each sentence)

13. _____

_____

14. _____

_____

15. _____

_____

16. _____

_____

Name _____   Perfect Score 30   My Score _____

UNIT I/LESSON 3

Recognizing Subjects, Verbs, and Direct Objects

▷ GUIDES *4, 5, 6*

Below each sentence write the subject, the verb or verb phrase, and the direct object, in that order. Subjects and direct objects may be compound. (Score: 30—3 for each sentence)

Example:

Do people in other nations love baseball?

people   *do love*   *baseball*

1. The Camagüeyanos won the Cuban national championship.

2. The men, women, and children of Camagüey line the streets.

3. Music and shouts of joy fill the air.

4. Jeeps carry the heroes along the Avenida Doble Villa.

5. Voices shout cheers and slogans, such as "Viva beisbol!"

6. In the Plaza de Caridad everyone welcomes the team.

7. Fans are shouting the names of Hernandez, Cruz, and Diaz.

8. This area's players have beaten teams from all over Cuba.

9. Will anyone ever forget the victory or the celebration?

10. But very soon many players will again take the field.

Name _____ Perfect Score 63   My Score _____

UNIT I/LESSON 4

Writing Subjective Complements

▷ GUIDE *8a, b*

Part I: Fill in each blank with a predicate noun. Punctuate each sentence. (Score: 18)

Example:

 An adult grizzly's weight may be 350 *kilograms.* _____

1. The grizzly bear is a powerful _____
2. One food of grizzly bears is _____
3. A weapon of the grizzly is its sharp _____
4. Once the American Northwest was wild _____
5. The ruler of the forest was the grizzly _____
6. To settlers, grizzly tracks were not a welcome _____
7. A state with many grizzly bears today is _____
8. The black bear is an intelligent _____
9. Wild honey is probably its favorite _____

Part II: Write the following sentences. In each sentence use the italicized word as a predicate adjective. (Score: 45—5 for each sentence)

Example:

 She is a *wise* judge. *The judge is wise. (or She is wise.)*

10. She is an *industrious* woman. _____
11. He was a very *artistic* man. _____
12. This is a *terrible* movie. _____
13. That was a *frightened* hiker. _____
14. Mine is a *green* coat. _____
15. You are a *clever* person. _____
16. That is a *valuable* ring. _____
17. Yours is a *large* apartment. _____
18. It was an extremely *hot* day. _____

8

Name _____ Perfect Score 55   My Score _____

UNIT I/LESSON 5

Recognizing Subjective Complements

▷ GUIDE *8a, b*

Part I: Underline each subject once and each subjective complement twice. On the line write the abbreviation that tells whether the subjective complement is a predicate noun *(PN)* or a predicate adjective *(PA)*. (Score: 45—3 for each sentence)

Example:

   Coin-operated <u>games</u> are <u><u>fun</u></u>.   *PA* _____

1. Today's favorites are the computer games. _____
2. Quick moves are helpful to a player. _____
3. Coin games are not new, of course. _____
4. Was Montague Redgrave the first pinball wizard? _____
5. 1871 was the date of his game's patent. _____
6. This game was mechanical, of course. _____
7. A mechanical racetrack game was an early favorite. _____
8. W. M. McManus of New York was its designer. _____
9. Fruit-vending machines are still popular today. _____
10. The inventor of these, Charles Fey, also was a game maker. _____
11. New versions of his machines are numerous in Nevada. _____
12. After 1900, Chicago became the center of the coin game business. _____
13. The tiny figures in the games were seldom pretty. _____
14. But the mechanical games were an inexpensive source of fun. _____
15. Today these old game machines are valuable. _____

Part II: Write two sentences that contain subjective complements. Underline each subjective complement. (Score: 10—5 for each sentence)

16. _____

_____

17. _____

_____

9

Name _____   Perfect Score 50   My Score _____

UNIT I/LESSON 6

Using Natural Word Order

▷ GUIDE 3

The natural order of words in a sentence can be changed so that the subject, verb, and other sentence elements are not in their usual positions. Write the following sentences in their natural order. (Score: 50—5 for each sentence)

Example:

Into the tall building marched the shy job hunter.

The shy job hunter marched into the tall building.

1. Into the elevator stepped the scared young man.

2. From every person there he thought he got stares.

3. This job he just had to have!

4. What he would say, he had practiced.

5. Through the heavy glass door he entered timidly.

6. All around him burst the sounds of people at work.

7. That office on the left he must enter.

8. Behind the big desk sat the personnel manager.

9. In a shaky voice he answered questions.

10. So impressed was she that she hired the young man.

Name _____   Perfect Score 42   My Score _____

UNIT I/LESSON 7

Choosing Appropriate Forms

▷ GUIDES *25a–d, 26, 29*

Part I: Underline the appropriate form in parentheses. (Score: 12)

(Is, Are) there any limits to Kitty O'Neil's talents? You may have (seen, saw) her on TV. She (does, do) stunts on many shows. Who (don't, doesn't) think that takes nerve?

But many of Kitty's accomplishments (isn't, aren't) stunts. The women's land speed record of 524.016 mph (is, are) hers. She (was, were) an AAU diving champion. Kitty (has, have) almost no hearing; yet she (is, are) a trained pianist and cellist. And what do you (thinks, think) of waterskiing at 104 mph?

If directors (call, calls) on Kitty O'Neil to play an American Indian character, it will be a fair choice. Ms. O'Neil (has, have) Cherokee ancestry.

Part II: Write a short paragraph about one of the most daring stunts you've seen on TV or in a movie. (Score: 25—10 for content, 5 for form, 10 for mechanics)

_____

_____

_____

_____

_____

_____

_____

_____

_____

▷ GUIDE *59 WORDSEARCH* (Score: 5) _____

1. scale   latitude   parallels   legend
2. diagram   chart   map

Discussion: Include the words in row 1 as you discuss how to use the information found in the plan named in WORDSEARCH.

Name   Perfect Score 34   My Score

UNIT I/LESSON 8

Capitalizing

▷ GUIDES *39a–g, 41*

Write appropriately each word that should be capitalized.

Example:

was he born in quincy, massachusetts?

Was   Quincy, Massachusetts

daniel hale williams was born in hollidaysburg, pennsylvania, in 1856. left an orphan at

twelve, he supported himself while he went to school. then, with the help of friends in

chicago, illinois, he entered northwestern medical school. daniel williams became a doctor

in june, 1883.

several years later he organized provident hospital in chicago. one summer night a man

with a wound in his heart was brought to the hospital. with the help of others, dr. williams

closed the wound and saved the man's life. the skillful black surgeon had performed the

first successful heart surgery. the year was 1893!

freedman's hospital in washington, d.c., was operated by the united states government.

dr. williams reorganized the hospital and made it one of the best of that time.

Name _____ Perfect Score 92   My Score _____

UNIT I/LESSON 9

Punctuating Sentences

▷ GUIDES *45, 48–53*

Part I: Place punctuation marks where they are needed. (Score: 52)

1. Tombstone Arizona was one of the wildest towns in the Old West
2. Clara who was Ed Schieffelin
3. Wasn't he a slow careful persistent prospector
4. Yes Schieffelin had searched in Oregon California and Nevada with little success
5. Then he began searching the hills near the San Pedro River in southern Arizona
6. What a hot dry empty area that was
7. How long Schieffelin searched without having any luck
8. Rattlesnakes Gila monsters and bandits lurked in the rocky canyons
9. Did Schieffelin say to a soldier that he would find something useful out there
10. Yes but what was the soldier's reply Clara
11. The soldier told Schieffelin that he would find one useful thing his own tombstone
12. Schieffelin however found a rich wide and promising vein of silver
13. Was the name of the claim the Tombstone an answer to the soldier's cruel reply
14. Soon the town of Tombstone Arizona was born
15. Toughnut Street Allen Street Fremont Street and Safford Street were laid out
16. What happened on Wednesday October 26 1881 at the O K Corral
17. Didn't Wyatt Earp his brothers and Doc Holliday duel Ike Clanton's men
18. "The town too tough to die" is still alive and kicking today Clara

Part II: Write three sentences about a historic building or town near you. Use a series in two sentences and an appositive in the other. (Score: 15—5 for each sentence)

19. _____

20. _____

21. _____

COMPOSITION: Write an article that describes a well-known local building or area of land. Include subjective complements in your description. (Score: 25—10 for content, 5 for form, 10 for mechanics)

Name _____ Perfect Score 45   My Score _____

UNIT I/LESSON 10

Review I

▷ GUIDES 1a, b, 2a, 4

Part I: Punctuate each group of words that is a sentence. Mark an X after each group of words that is not a sentence. Underline the subject in each sentence. (Score: 9)

1. American bison once roamed the prairies
2. Known a buffalo
3. Supplied food, clothing, shelter
4. Bison were killed at an alarming rate
5. Settlers shot many bison for sport
6. Laws to protect bison

▷ GUIDES 39a–g, 41

Part II: Underline each word that should be capitalized. (Score: 16)

7. on april 1, 1981, we left for yellowstone national park.
8. did cara go with you to lincoln, nebraska?
9. dr. s. laura townsend started her practice at the harvard medical center.

▷ GUIDES 6, 8a, b

Part III: Underline each subject once and each subjective complement or direct object twice. On the line write the abbreviation that tells whether the word underlined twice is a predicate noun, *PN*; a predicate adjective, *PA*; or a direct object, *DO*.
(Score: 15—3 for each sentence)

10. Rachel is our kicker. _____
11. Rachel kicked the ball thirty-eight yards for a field goal. _____
12. She is the best in our league. _____
13. Rachel won an award from the sportswriters. _____
14. We are very happy for her. _____

▷ GUIDES 25a–d, 26, 29

Part IV: Underline the appropriate form in parentheses. (Score: 5)

15. Cortney (has, have) plenty of tickets for the concert in Chicago.
16. We have (drove, driven) six hundred miles in the last two days.
17. (Aren't, Isn't) you getting tired?
18. Kyle and Cortney (is, are) going but you (isn't, aren't).

14

Name _____   Perfect Score 28   My Score _____

UNIT II/LESSON 11

Recognizing Simple and Compound Sentences

▷ GUIDES *9, 10*

Part I: On the line after each sentence write whether it is *simple* or *compound*. In every compound sentence underline each complete thought and put parentheses around the conjunction.

Examples:

    Most people hope for peaceful lives. *simple* _____

    <u>They worry about disaster,</u> (but) <u>they do not prepare for it.</u> *compound* _____

1. Mount Vesuvius is probably the world's most famous volcano. _____

2. It rises 4,000 feet above the Bay of Naples in Italy. _____

3. In 79 A.D. the mountain erupted violently, and the city of Pompeii was buried under 50 feet of ash and stone. _____

4. Mount Saint Helens is the most famous volcano in the United States. _____

5. It used to rise 9,677 feet above sea level. _____

6. Mount Saint Helens is near Vancouver, Washington, and it is part of the Cascade Mountains. _____

7. The volcano first came back to life on March 27, 1980. _____

8. On May 18, 1980, the volcano erupted full force. _____

9. The explosion blew 1,300 feet off the top of the volcano, and ash and rock flowed at 200 miles an hour down the mountain. _____

10. The ash and rock shot over 60,000 feet in the air. _____

11. Almost everything for 20 miles north and west of the volcano was destroyed. _____

12. Everything near the volcano was covered by up to 200 feet of ash, and ash blew east and south all the way across the United States. _____

13. Mount Saint Helens's eruption was terrifying and destructive, but it was a small eruption compared to Mount Vesuvius. _____

15

Name _____ Perfect Score 45   My Score _____

UNIT II/LESSON 12

Writing Compound Sentences

▷ GUIDE *37a, b*

Use the conjunctions *and*, *but*, or *or* to combine two short sentences into one compound sentence. Place a comma before the conjunction. (Score: 45—5 for each sentence)

Example:

We have made progress. We can be proud of much of our modern life-style.

We have made progress, and we can be proud of much of our modern life-style.

1. There were wise people in ancient times. They understood life, too. _____
_____

2. Their statements were made long ago. Their wisdom is apparent today. _____
_____

3. Cicero lived 2,000 years ago. He was a famous Roman writer. _____
_____

4. Cicero was an orator and a politician. He is remembered for his writings. _____
_____

5. He wrote about people's foolish ideas. Time has not proved him wrong. _____
_____

6. People try to get ahead. Some do so at the expense of others. _____
_____

7. Many things cannot be changed. We worry about them anyway. _____
_____

8. We want others to agree with us. We are unwilling to change. _____
_____

9. Do Cicero's words apply to us? Have we risen above foolish ideas? _____
_____

16

Name _____ Perfect Score 40   My Score _____

UNIT II/LESSON 13

Using Compound Elements

▷ GUIDE *37c*

Combine the sentences below by forming compound elements. (Score: 40—5 for each sentence)

Examples:

Augusta Rogers was an inventor. William Addis was another.

Augusta Rogers and William Addis were inventors. (compound subject)

Augusta Rogers was from Brooklyn. She invented many new things.

Augusta Rogers was from Brooklyn and invented many new things. (compound predicate)

One of her inventions is important. It is well known.

One of her inventions is important and well known. (compound subjective complement)

1. Augusta Rogers invented the automobile heater. She patented it. _____

2. Her invention did not use fire. It did not cause fire. _____

3. Around 1770, William Addis broke British law. He started a riot. _____

4. He was put in prison. Other people were put in prison. _____

5. Life in prison was very dull. Life in prison was very disagreeable. _____

6. Every day he washed his face. He cleaned his teeth with a rag. _____

7. The ancients had used rags. Everyone else had used rags to clean teeth. _____

8. William Addis invented the toothbrush. He became an overnight success. _____

17

Name _____ Perfect Score 60   My Score _____

UNIT II/*LESSON 14*

Combining Sentences

▷ GUIDES *10, 37a–c*

First write a compound sentence by combining the two short sentences. Then combine the short sentences using a compound element. (Score: 60—5 for each sentence)

Examples:

    Is it an artery? Is it a vein? (two short sentences)

    Is it an artery, or is it a vein? (compound sentence)

    Is it an artery or a vein? (compound element)

1. Arteries carry blood through the body. Veins also carry blood. _____
_____
_____

2. The heart is like a machine. It pumps blood constantly. _____
_____
_____

3. It pumps blood into the arteries. It gets blood from the veins. _____
_____
_____

4. Blood carries food to the body. It carries oxygen to the body. _____
_____
_____

5. We need oxygen constantly. We can die from lack of "fuel." _____
_____
_____

6. The heart, blood, and lungs never rest. They work less during sleep. _____
_____
_____

Name   Perfect Score 55   My Score

UNIT II/*LESSON 15*

Punctuating Sentences

▷ GUIDES *2a–d, 48, 50–53*

Part I: Punctuate each sentence. (Score: 40)

1. Is the Fahrenheit scale the best way to tell temperature or should we change
2. Water freezes at 32° Fahrenheit and it boils at 212° F
3. Britain the U S and other English-speaking countries often use this measure
4. The rest of the world however uses the Celsius scale
5. This scale also called the centigrade scale is easy to use
6. On this simple scale water freezes at 0° C and it boils at 100° C
7. Are the freezing and boiling points of water separated by only 100 degrees
8. Yes they are and this feature makes the scale easy to use
9. How simple that must be
10. Yes it is simple and it is used in scientific work
11. The Celsius scale is used in science engineering and many other fields
12. Old habits of course are hard to change
13. Slowly inch by inch little by little we are changing
14. The change will affect our way of measuring temperature
15. On February 10 1964 our National Bureau of Standards started using the new system

Part II: Write two sentences about the difficulty of changing old habits. Use a compound element in one sentence. (Score: 10—5 for each sentence)

16. _____

17. _____

▷ GUIDE *59 WORDSEARCH* (Score: 5)

1. Asia   Europe   Africa   North America
2. continent   province   republic

Discussion: Include the words in row 1 as you discuss how the area of land named in WORDSEARCH divides the world.

Name _____   Perfect Score 50   My Score _____

UNIT II/LESSON 16

Forming Plurals and Possessives

▷ GUIDES *13, 14, 20*

Part I: Write five sentences. In each sentence use the plural form of the noun in parentheses. (Score: 25—5 for each sentence)

1. (fly) _____
   _____

2. (woman) _____
   _____

3. (crash) _____
   _____

4. (piano) _____
   _____

5. (story) _____
   _____

Part II: Write five sentences. In each sentence use the possessive form of the word in parentheses. (Score: 25—5 for each sentence)

6. (JoAnne) _____
   _____

7. (we) _____
   _____

8. (engines) _____
   _____

9. (brothers) _____
   _____

10. (she) _____
    _____

Name _____   Perfect Score 29   My Score _____

UNIT II/LESSON 17

Using Nouns as Indirect Objects

▷ GUIDE 7

Part I: On the line after each sentence write the noun or nouns used as an indirect object. (Score: 9)

Example: Books offer people an escape from daily life. *people* _____

1. Agatha Christie gives readers an exciting escape. _____
2. Her detective stories brought Ms. Christie fame. _____
3. Stores have sold customers more than 300 million copies. _____
4. She gave fiction two famous detectives. _____
5. Hercule Poirot brings his cases the skills of analysis. _____
6. Miss Marple offers our minds and imaginations her knowledge and her understanding of people. _____
7. She took publishers her first efforts. _____
8. They gave Ms. Christie encouraging words but nothing more. _____
9. Her first successful novel showed the world her potential. _____

Part II: Write each of the following sentences so that it contains an indirect object. (Score: 20—5 for each sentence)

Example: Agatha Christie's first novel showed Hercule Poirot to the world.
   Agatha Christie's first novel showed the world Hercule Poirot.

10. *The Mysterious Affair at Style* gives exciting reading to many. _____
_____

11. Agatha Christie's works give pleasure to her admirers. _____
_____

12. Her travels provided some unusual settings for these works. _____
_____

13. All this has won large audiences for Agatha Christie. _____
_____

21

Name _____   Perfect Score 43   My Score _____

UNIT II/LESSON 18

Recognizing Nouns

▷ GUIDES *3, 4, 6, 7, 8a, 12, 13, 14*

Underline every noun used as a subject, predicate noun, indirect object, or direct object. On the line below the noun, tell how each is used. (Score: 38)

Example:

<u>Deserts</u> have always interested <u>people</u>.

subject   *direct object*

1. The desert is a fascinating place.

2. It is a harsh but beautiful land.

3. The early sunlight gives the sand and rocks a red glow.

4. Later the heat and glare create a furnace.

5. The rattlesnake is a common desert creature.

6. Does it give every living thing a chill feeling?

7. Sunset offers the traveler a great contrast.

8. Nightfall changes the desert landscape.

▷ GUIDE *59 WORDSEARCH* (Score: 5) _____

1. pulp   trees   cotton   cellulose
2. wool   paper   nylon

Discussion: Include the words in row 1 as you discuss different ways the product in WORDSEARCH is manufactured.

22

Name _____ Perfect Score 97   My Score _____

UNIT II/*LESSON 19*

Using Capitalization and Punctuation

▷ GUIDES *2, 14, 39a–c, e, 41, 45, 48, 52*

Write the following paragraph. Use appropriate capitalization and punctuation. (Score: 67)

the united states won its freedom from great britain but the two nations were soon at war again the fighting lasted more than two years and the struggle became known as the war of 1812 the british the canadians and their indian allies won many battles fortunately the americans won some victories on january 8 1815 a major battle was fought at new orleans louisiana british troops led by general sir edward packenham attacked smaller american forces led by general andrew jackson the british attacked in closed ranks the americans stayed hidden the order to jacksons troops was don't fire till you see the whites of their eyes over two thousand british troops were killed but only 13 americans died the battle however came *after* the treaty was signed

_____

_____

_____

_____

_____

_____

_____

_____

_____

_____

COMPOSITION: Imagine that you have invented the electric blanket. Use short, simple sentences to describe the advantages of the blanket. Then combine the simple sentences into compound sentences and write an advertisement for your invention. (Score: 30—10 for contents, 5 for form, 15 for mechanics)

Name _____   Perfect Score 44   My Score _____

UNIT II/LESSON 20

Review II

▷ GUIDE *14*

Part I: Write the possessive form of each word. (Score: 4)

1. sidewalk _____   3. women _____

2. pitchers _____   4. sheep _____

▷ GUIDE *4*

Part II: Write a sentence using two nouns as the compound subject. (Score: 5)

5. _____

▷ GUIDE *5*

Part III: Write a sentence using two verbs as a compound element. (Score: 5)

6. _____

▷ GUIDE *7*

Part IV: Use each word in parentheses in a sentence with an indirect object. (Score: 10—5 for each sentence)

7. (offered) _____

8. (sent) _____

▷ GUIDE *6*

Part V: Use each word in parentheses in a sentence with a direct object. (Score: 10—5 for each sentence)

9. (slam) _____

10. (ate) _____

▷ GUIDE *8a, b*

Part VI: Use the word in parentheses in a sentence with a subjective complement. (Score: 5)

11. (was) _____

▷ GUIDE *10*

Part VII: Write a compound sentence. (Score: 5)

12. _____

24

Name _____   Perfect Score 72   My Score _____

UNIT III/LESSON 21

Identifying Prepositions and Prepositional Phrases

▷ GUIDE *36a, b*

Part I: Place parentheses around each prepositional phrase. Underline each preposition. (Score: 52)

Example:

We drove the car (<u>from</u> Tulsa) (<u>to</u> Dallas) (<u>without</u> a stop) (<u>for</u> gas).

At the age of ten I became interested in cars. We had an old car on blocks in the backyard. My parents let me work on it. I would rise at seven in the morning and play with the valves and carburetor. By age sixteen I had rebuilt engines from a dozen cars. I took a job in a garage and worked on weekends and during the summer. I saved $250 in six months and bought a sedan with a cracked engine block. At the end of a year of hard work, it was ready. I towed it from my backyard to a local strip and entered the time trials. That car had a terrible time in the quarter mile, but I got quite a thrill from my ride down the dusty strip. It was a start, and someday, with luck, I'll break the land speed record at Bonneville!

Part II: Write three sentences about something you enjoy doing in your spare time. Use some of these words in prepositional phrases: *from, in, on, at, with, during, between, by, across, after.* (Score: 15—5 for each sentence)

1. _____

2. _____

3. _____

▷ GUIDE *59 WORDSEARCH* (Score: 5)
1. Peking   Mandarin   Sinkiang   Yangtze
2. Rhodesia   China   Egypt

Discussion: Include the words in row 1 as you discuss the history of the country named in WORDSEARCH.

25

Name _____ Perfect Score 58   My Score _____

UNIT III/LESSON 22

Identifying Nouns and Pronouns

▷ GUIDES *12, 15a*

Part I: Underline the nouns in the following sentences. (Score: 35)

1. Jim lost a book last week.
2. Greg and Anne say that Jim loses books all the time.
3. Maybe Jim lost this book on purpose.
4. The book was about how to build your memory.
5. Brent found a lunchbox belonging to Jim under the stairs.
6. Brent ate the sandwiches before he returned the lunchbox to Jim.
7. Another time Jim lost Lorre at a concert.
8. Jim felt foolish when Lorre arrived at the house in a taxi.
9. The librarians will charge Jim ten dollars for the book.
10. Maybe that expense will improve his memory.

Part II: Underline the pronouns that have been substituted for some of the underlined nouns above. (Other words may also have been eliminated when the pronoun was substituted.) (Score: 23)

11. He lost it last week.
12. They say that he loses them all the time.
13. Maybe he lost it on purpose.
14. It was about how to build your memory.
15. He found it under the stairs.
16. He ate them before he returned it to him.
17. Another time he lost her at a concert.
18. He felt foolish when she arrived at the house in a taxi.
19. They will charge him ten dollars for it.
20. Maybe it will improve his memory.

Name _____   Perfect Score 32   My Score _____

UNIT III/*LESSON 23*

Identifying Kinds of Pronouns

▷ GUIDES *15–17*

Part I: Underline each personal pronoun. (Score: 6)

1. We will be leaving soon for the airport.
2. Our friends should arrive at 3:05.
3. We hope that they will be on time.
4. They are going to stay with us for a week.

Part II: Underline each compound personal pronoun. (Score: 5)

5. Marsha changed the oil herself.
6. I know that you are disappointed in yourself.
7. Stan and Jake left by themselves.
8. I wrote the story myself.
9. We made the movie ourselves.

Part III: Underline each interrogative pronoun. (Score: 5)

10. Who will carry the soda?
11. Which do you prefer?
12. Whose are these books?
13. What is your address?
14. Whom did you ask for?

Part IV: Underline each pronoun. On the line write whether the pronoun is *personal, compound personal,* or *interrogative.* (Score: 16)

15. Kelly finished the painting by herself.   _____
16. The newspaper gave us a good write-up.   _____
17. Who can come to the party?   _____
18. Which is the highway to Chicago?   _____
19. You can find the house easily.   _____
20. Todd talks to himself.   _____
21. What is the matter?   _____
22. Will she be here on time?   _____

27

Name _____   Perfect Score 25   My Score _____

UNIT III/LESSON 24

Identifying Kinds of Pronouns

▷ GUIDES *18–20*

Part I: Underline each demonstrative pronoun. (Score: 4)
1. These go in the cabinet.
2. Who made this?
3. You may take those outside.
4. Who brought that?

Part II: Underline each indefinite pronoun. (Score: 5)
5. Anyone may attend the concert free.
6. Is someone using the barbells?
7. All of the students passed driver's education.
8. There are some under my desk.
9. None of the students missed cooking class.

Part III: Underline each possessive pronoun. (Score: 6)
10. Is that bike yours or mine?
11. It's his bike that was run over.
12. Ours are still in the bike rack.
13. Jamie is leaving for her vacation.
14. I will take mine in two weeks.

Part IV: Underline each pronoun. On the line beside each sentence write whether the pronoun is *demonstrative*, *indefinite*, or *possessive*. (Score: 10)

15. How long does Dawn plan to work on that? _____
16. Where will his grandmother live? _____
17. All of the helmets are safe. _____
18. Are these ready to go? _____
19. Cindy likes her new job. _____

28

Name _____   Perfect Score 20   My Score _____

UNIT III/*LESSON 25*

Recognizing Pronouns as Sentence Elements

▷ GUIDES *8a, 15b–d*

The pronoun in italics may be a subject, a direct object, an indirect object, an object of a preposition, or a predicate nominative. On the line write the sentence element.

1. *I* have always liked monster movies. _____
2. My sister took *me* to my first one when I was six. _____
3. *We* sat in the first row. _____
4. I went with *her* to the movies every Saturday. _____
5. *I* would scream at the monsters and she would laugh. _____
6. Once, the kid beside *me* poured soda on my feet. _____
7. I gave *him* the same treatment. _____
8. My sister yelled at *me* when we got home. _____
9. *I* saw *Jaws II* and thought it was the best movie ever. _____
10. It scared *me* half to death. _____
11. The new version of *King Kong* didn't scare *me*. _____
12. The movie gave *me* a sideache because I laughed so hard at it. _____
13. It was *he* who kept knocking down the walls of the villages. _____
14. Every time I laughed, my sister would frown at *me*. _____
15. Finally, in the middle of the movie, *she* took me home. _____
16. Later, I was allowed to go to the movies by *myself*. _____
17. Sometimes *I* would watch a movie three times in a row. _____
18. After the third time, I could almost recite *it* from memory. _____
19. Monster movies still seem to *me* to be the best kind. _____
20. I'm not a child anymore, but some of them still give *me* a chill. _____

Name _____ Perfect Score 34   My Score _____

UNIT III/LESSON 26

Learning about Pronoun Agreement

▷ GUIDE *15e*

Part I: Underline the pronoun or pronouns in each of the following sentences. Write the antecedent on the line. (Score: 23)

Example:

Roz knows her responsibilities. *Roz* _____

1. The nurses make their rounds several times a day. _____
2. The doctor said that she would examine the patient. _____
3. Each doctor has his or her own patients. _____
4. Art and Marie think that Dr. Adams is the best doctor on their ward. _____
5. Greta wants Dr. Abraham to be her doctor. _____
6. Aides must work night shifts just as their associates do. _____
7. Dr. Adams hopes to have her own practice soon. _____
8. Most doctors here want their own practices. _____
9. Each doctor will someday do as he or she wishes. _____
10. But all doctors here will keep their current jobs for some time. _____

Part II: Fill in each blank with an appropriate pronoun. (Score: 11)

11. Art doesn't enjoy _____ job as an orderly.
12. Someday he may be a doctor, as _____ sister is.
13. The patients praise her for _____ kindness.
14. Each patient has _____ or _____ favorite nurse.
15. All patients express _____ liking for Nurse McDonald.
16. Some of them have told _____ doctors about Art.
17. They say he is _____ favorite orderly.
18. Art has filled out _____ applications to medical schools.
19. Will he be accepted by the school of _____ choice?
20. He will keep _____ job until he is accepted.

30

Name _____   Perfect Score 50   My Score _____

UNIT III/*LESSON 27*

Using Pronouns

▷ GUIDES *15–20*

Write sentences using pronouns as indicated in parentheses. (Score: 50—5 for each sentence)

Example:

(a pronoun as an indirect object)   *Clancy gave him two dimes for a nickel.*

1. (two pronouns as a compound subject) _____

2. (two pronouns as a compound object of a preposition) _____

3. (two pronouns as a compound direct object) _____

4. (two pronouns as a compound indirect object) _____

5. (the demonstrative pronoun *these*) _____

6. (the compound personal pronoun *yourself*) _____

7. (the indefinite pronoun *each*) _____

8. (the interrogative pronoun *what*) _____

9. (the possessive pronoun *its*) _____

10. (the personal pronoun *us*) _____

Name _____ Perfect Score 22   My Score _____

UNIT III/LESSON 28

Using a Dictionary to Find Information

▷ GUIDE 57

Use a dictionary to see whether the statements below are true or false. Write *yes* or *no* on the line. (Score: 17)

Example:

    A *portico* is a place where ships dock.   *no*

1. You might play cards with a *cheetah*.
2. An *ironmonger* is a stiff-haired breed of dog.
3. A *paragon* is a good model.
4. You could be expected to swim in a *pongee*.
5. *Populace* is a fancy trimming for dresses.
6. It would be hard to get money from a *skinflint*.
7. The skin of a certain animal is *oxide*.
8. A *skulk* is an animal with a large head.
9. *Culpable* means deserving of blame.
10. A *tun* is measured in gallons.
11. One kind of orange fruit is a *tangible*.
12. *Hepatica* is a sickness that damages the liver.
13. A *turban* is a kind of engine in a power plant.
14. A *marten* is a black bird.
15. The second syllable of *pamphlet* begins with the sound *f*.
16. A kind of stringed instrument is called a *mandible*.
17. You might be hurt by *mandibles*.

▷ GUIDE 59 *WORDSEARCH* (Score: 5) _____

1. snorkel   fins   mouthpiece   wet suit
2. skin diving   deep-sea fishing   surfing

Discussion: Include the words in row 1 as you discuss the safety rules for the sport named in WORDSEARCH.

Name _____   Perfect Score 57   My Score _____

UNIT III/LESSON 29

Choosing Appropriate Forms

▷ GUIDES *15, 17, 20, 26, 29, 33c, 36*

Part I: Underline the appropriate word in parentheses. (Score: 17)

1. Scientists have (knew, known) for some time that blue whales are disappearing.
2. (Those, Them) mammoth creatures are the largest animals that have ever lived.
3. This whale may measure a hundred feet (between, in between) nose and tail.
4. (It's, Its) heart alone may weigh more than a thousand pounds.
5. (Whose, Who's) fault is it that these whales are disappearing?
6. Whalers should know that the fault is (there's, theirs).
7. Since 1865 whalers have (gone, went) hunting with whaling guns.
8. (Between, Among) 1900 and today, whalers have killed over 300,000 blue whales.
9. They have (took, taken) 30,000 whales in one year.
10. Enormous profits have been made (off, from) the blue whale.
11. Virtually every part of the whale goes (in, into) valuable products.
12. Regulations have been (wrote, written) for the protection of the whale.
13. Scientists fear that this action was (took, taken) too late.
14. They think that fatal damage has already been (did, done).
15. In 1908 an explorer (saw, seen) hundreds of whales in an Antarctic bay.
16. Large numbers of these creatures are (saw, seen) no more.
17. Within just a few years the gigantic blue whale may be (saw, seen) no more.

Part II: Write three sentences. In each sentence use a preposition with the pronouns in parentheses. (Score: 15—5 for each sentence)

18. (him and me) _____

19. (yours and ours) _____

20. (him and her) _____

COMPOSITION: Write a review of a magazine article or book you have read recently. Make sure that each pronoun agrees with its antecedent. (Score: 25—10 for content, 5 for form, 10 for mechanics)

Name _____ Perfect Score 50   My Score _____

UNIT III/*LESSON 30*

Review III

▷ GUIDE *36a, b*

Part I: Write five sentences. In each sentence use the preposition in parentheses. (Score: 25—5 for each sentence)

1. (between) _____
   _____

2. (off) _____
   _____

3. (at) _____
   _____

4. (through) _____
   _____

5. (in) _____
   _____

▷ GUIDE *15*

Part II: Write five sentences. In each sentence use the word or words in parentheses. (Score: 25—5 for each sentence)

6. (Meg and them) _____
   _____

7. (its) _____
   _____

8. (Meg and I) _____
   _____

9. (their) _____
   _____

10. (everyone) _____
    _____

34

Name _____ Perfect Score 72 My Score _____

UNIT IV/LESSON 31

Identifying Adjectives

▷ GUIDE 33a–f

Underline the adjectives in the following sentences. Below each adjective name the noun it modifies. More than one adjective may modify the same noun. Do not underline articles. (Score: 72—1 for each adjective and 1 for each noun)

Example:

Napoleon I, the <u>powerful</u> emperor, knew the <u>great</u> value of <u>good</u>, <u>wholesome</u> food.
  emperor   value   food   food

1. This fiery, brilliant leader gave us the first effective container for fresh food.

2. In 1795 he offered a large sum as first prize in a special contest.

3. He asked for the invention of a new way for preserving fresh food.

4. Every clever French inventor must have wanted that fat prize.

5. Nicolas Appert worked for many years on this difficult problem.

6. He partially cooked fresh foods and put them into sturdy glass bottles.

7. Then he closed the warm, steamy bottles with cork stoppers.

8. The full bottles were plunged into a large pot of hot water.

9. This simple, effective method killed harmful bacteria.

10. So this bright, patient Parisian won the rich prize.

35

Name _____ Perfect Score 33   My Score _____

UNIT IV/LESSON 32

Recognizing Predicate Adjectives

▷ GUIDE *8b*

On the line after each sentence write the predicate adjective and the noun or pronoun it modifies. A sentence may have more than one predicate adjective.

Example:

Giant tortoises look strong and noble.

strong, noble tortoises

1. Once these reptiles were numerous throughout the world. _____
2. Slowly their numbers became smaller. _____
3. The tortoises were existent only on a few ocean islands. _____
4. The Galápagos Islands are isolated. _____
5. Survival for Galápagos tortoises was not difficult until after 1535. _____
6. Then sailors became aware of these rocky islands. _____
7. Sailors can become weary, bored, and hungry for fresh food. _____
8. A stop at the Galápagos Islands was perfect for rest and refreshment. _____
9. Tortoise meat is delicious. _____
10. The large animals were very slow. _____
11. Tortoises could be kept healthy on the ships. _____
12. The cruelty of some crews seems incredible. _____
13. Tortoises soon were very scarce on many islands. _____
14. The story of the tortoise's decline is long and sad. _____
15. Their extinction appears quite possible. _____

36

Name _____   Perfect Score 40   My Score _____

UNIT IV/LESSON 33

Combining Sentences

▷ GUIDE *8b*

Combine the short sentences by placing each predicate adjective before the noun it modifies. (Score: 35—5 for each sentence)

Examples:

    That coin is shiny. It's smaller than a dime.

    That shiny coin is smaller than a dime.

    Is that a one-dollar gold piece? Is it rare?

    Is that a rare one-dollar gold piece?

1. Its mint mark is tiny. It is below the wreath.

   _____

2. Charlotte, North Carolina, once had a United States mint. The mint was small.

   _____

3. Did the mint produce quantities of gold coins? Were the quantities small?

   _____

4. Its coins are valuable. They are prized by collectors.

   _____

5. The attic was dusty. Was it filled with old boxes?

   _____

6. I found a coin purse there. It looked worn.

   _____

7. It held an 1853-c one-dollar gold piece! The coin was elegant!

   _____

▷ GUIDE *59 WORDSEARCH* (Score: 5) _____

1. pit   venom   fang   coil
2. alligator   snake   shark

Discussion: Include the words in row 1 as you discuss the different varieties of the animal named in WORDSEARCH.

Name _____ Perfect Score 38   My Score _____

UNIT IV/LESSON 34

Recognizing Adverbs

▷ GUIDES *22, 34a*

Part I: In each sentence draw one line under the verb or verb phrase and draw two lines under the adverb or adverbs that modify it. (Score: 28—1 for each verb or verb phrase and 1 for each adverb)

Example:

A fairy-tale world <u>is</u> <u><u>securely</u></u> <u>wrapped</u> in the mountains.

1. The country is officially ruled by a prince.
2. Prince Franz Josef II has ruled quietly for over forty years.
3. The prince and his family live simply in a castle.
4. The people long ago abolished their army.
5. Most citizens are productively employed.
6. The country's 26,000 people live happily.
7. The country, Liechtenstein, is approximately the size of Washington, D.C.
8. The people of Liechtenstein primarily speak German.
9. Liechtenstein is probably best known for its beautiful postage stamps.
10. Industry is limited mainly to tools and false teeth.
11. This country of highlands and mountains warmly welcomes skiers from all over the world.
12. Today, women do not vote in national elections.
13. This situation may change soon.

Part II: Write two sentences. In each sentence use the adverb in parentheses. (Score: 10—5 for each sentence)

14. (always) _____

_____

15. (never) _____

_____

Name _____   Perfect Score 51   My Score _____

UNIT IV/LESSON 35

Identifying Adverbs

▷ GUIDE *34b, c*

Part I: Underline the adverb that modifies an adjective or another adverb. On the first line after the sentence write the word the adverb modifies. On the second line, tell whether that word is an adjective or adverb. (Score: 36—3 for each sentence)

Examples:

This is the <u>most</u> elegant disco in the city.	*elegant*	*adj.*
Each weekend the dancers dress <u>more</u> stylishly.	*stylishly*	*adv.*

1. Admission to this disco was more expensive. _____ _____
2. Was the music incredibly loud? _____ _____
3. Flashing colored lights were almost everywhere. _____ _____
4. I could just barely see through the dry-ice smoke. _____ _____
5. An extremely large artificial palm stood in a corner. _____ _____
6. I wore my new gold velvet jacket very proudly. _____ _____
7. It was certainly noticeable against the silver wallpaper. _____ _____
8. The dance floor was completely transparent. _____ _____
9. Is there a somewhat similar disco in your area? _____ _____
10. We were there for nearly three hours. _____ _____
11. The time passed incredibly fast. _____ _____
12. We were not quite prepared for the cold of the night. _____ _____

Part II: Write three sentences. In each sentence use the adverb indicated to modify an adjective or another adverb. (Score: 15—5 for each sentence)

13. (very) _____

_____

14. (most) _____

_____

15. (hardly) _____

_____

Name _____ Perfect Score 32   My Score _____

UNIT IV/LESSON 36

Recognizing Prepositional Phrases

▷ GUIDE 36c, d

Part I: Underline each prepositional phrase used as an adjective. On the line write the noun that the phrase modifies. (Score: 16—2 for each sentence)

Example:

   The face <u>in the mirror</u> was strange indeed.   *face* _____

1. The hair of the detective was now white.   _____
2. What was the reason for this odd disguise?   _____
3. The owner of the Silver Scream Waxworks had hired her.   _____
4. Someone had been melting the faces of his wax figures.   _____
5. The task of the detective was not easy.   _____
6. How would she manage the capture of this mad torcher?   _____
7. The guard in the building had always arrived too late.   _____
8. The detective chose a pedestal beside a wax Humphrey Bogart.   _____

Part II: Underline each prepositional phrase used as an adverb. On the line write the verb or verb phrase that the prepositional phrase modifies. (Score: 16—2 for each sentence)

Example:

   She stood quite still <u>for an hour</u>.   *stood* _____

9. Then a light appeared above the wax Elizabeth I.   _____
10. A shadow was creeping silently down the aisle.   _____
11. It suddenly raised a hissing torch toward the detective's face! _____
12. From the pedestal the disguised detective leaped!   _____
13. She grabbed the torcher with an iron grip.   _____
14. The detective was shocked by the torcher's face.   _____
15. To her surprise she had caught the waxworks owner!   _____
16. Never in her life had she had a case this strange.   _____

Name _____   Perfect Score 53   My Score _____

UNIT IV/LESSON 37

Identifying Prepositional Phrases

▷ GUIDE *36c, d*

Part I: Underline the prepositional phrase in each sentence. Place parentheses around the noun or verb the phrase modifies. On the line tell whether the phrase is used as an adjective or as an adverb. (Score: 33—3 for each sentence)

Examples:

 The typewriter (was invented) <u>in the last century</u>. *adverb*

 Modern offices may use (hundreds) <u>of typewriters</u>. *adjective*

1. Shortly after the Civil War a usable typewriter was invented. _____
2. It was the invention of Christopher Sholes. _____
3. He had been an editor for a Wisconsin newspaper. _____
4. He and two other people got a patent on the typewriter. _____
5. Through the years, typewriters have been improved. _____
6. How much we depend on them today! _____
7. No office could operate without one. _____
8. Writers of every kind must record their words. _____
9. Many have switched to word processors. _____
10. The keys of Sholes's typewriter resembled piano keys. _____
11. Modern typewriters would be a surprise to the inventor. _____

Part II: Write two sentences using the prepositional phrase in parentheses. In the first sentence use the phrase as an adjective. In the second sentence use the phrase as an adverb. (Score: 20—5 for each sentence)

 (on the typewriter)

12. _____
13. _____

 (in an office)

14. _____
15. _____

Name Perfect Score 35 My Score

UNIT IV/LESSON 38

Correcting a Paragraph

▷ GUIDES *15a, 29–31, 34d, 35*

Draw a line through any inappropriate word. If it needs to be replaced, write an appropriate word above. (Score: 30)

Example:

very eager
My friends Sergei and Elnora are ~~real eagerly~~ to work.

Neither of them has no experience. But their readily too learn. Sergei heared about a training program last week. He signed up as quick as he could. He maybe become a forklift operator. Its not easy to rise pallets without upsetting them. But Sergei don't worry none about learning. And he ain't never been no quitter. Elnora maybe have a job in a tire warehouse. If you was to ask her, she would tell you proud of her skills. If she can't be learned to be a supervisor, nobody can't. Elnora's not afraid of no hard work, neither. He arms and legs is strong from exercising regular. She never sets down when theirs work to do. My friends hope to begin work immediate. They may not be successfully this week, but there surely to be hired in the near future.

▷ GUIDE **59** *WORDSEARCH* (Score: 5)

1. shaft strip excavation furnace
2. wood oil coal

Discussion: Include the words in row 1 as you discuss the different uses of the resource named in WORDSEARCH.

UNIT IV/LESSON 39

Using Capitalization and Punctuation

▷ GUIDES *39a, b, 45, 46, 51, 52, 54b*

Write the paragraph correctly. (Score: 71)

    in the southwestern town of okemah oklahoma woody guthrie was born in 1912 he was a poor boy with itchy feet and great talents during his youth he rode freight trains all over the united states his uncle had taught him to play the guitar and his guitar was always with him he composed songs about penniless travelers about ordinary people and even about the bonneville dam he truly traveled from new york to california he wrote a book about himself too called bound for glory he was just becoming famous when he became very ill he spent the last fifteen years of his life in a hospital however people today sing his songs more than ever hasn't everyone heard his song this land is your land the okemah library in his hometown has paid him a tribute his music is recorded in the library of congress a power plant in the pacific northwest was named in his honor woody guthrie will be remembered by the country he loved

COMPOSITION: Describe for a radio audience a sports event you have seen or taken part in. (Score: 25—10 for content, 5 for form, 10 for mechanics)

Name _____ Perfect Score 65   My Score _____

UNIT IV/LESSON 40

Review IV
▷ GUIDES *2a, b, d, 48–52*

Part I: Punctuate these sentences correctly. (Score: 16)
1. Ronald Reagan was inaugurated president on Jan 20 1981 in Washington D C
2. This event was celebrated with a parade formal dinners balls and speeches
3. Of course many people attended the festivities
4. Jon did you get to go
5. No but it must have been exciting

▷ GUIDES *15e, 25a, b, 26, 27, 29, 30, 32, 39a, b, d, g, 41*

Part II: Circle any word that should be capitalized. Cross out any inappropriate word and write the appropriate word above it. (Score: 24)

6. casey done all of he work on tuesday.
7. the greensboro high school band marches in the parade last week.
8. mrs. jenner ain't learned me nothing.
9. zac and jerry was laying down when he should have went to work.
10. i seen you when you was racing at daytona.

▷ GUIDES *33a, b, d, 34a–d*

Part III: Underline each adjective once and each adverb twice. Do not underline articles. (Score: 14)

11. He rose slowly and calmly walked toward the angry dog.
12. The dark, silent night was shattered by a deadly explosion.
13. The completely incompetent barber cut Maria's hair so unevenly that it wouldn't lie flat for weeks.
14. Beat the eggs thoroughly with a wire whip.

▷ GUIDE *36*

Part IV: Underline once each prepositional phrase used as an adjective. Underline twice each prepositional phrase used as an adverb. (Score: 11)

15. The spare tire is in the trunk.
16. When you go to the kitchen, please bring me a glass of milk.
17. Press the leaf between two pages of a heavy book.
18. Among the stars, Katharine Hepburn is one of the brightest.
19. She ran into the house carrying a bunch of flowers.
20. I need a pair of shoes with rubber soles.

Name _____   Perfect Score 40   My Score _____

UNIT V/LESSON 41

Writing Verb Forms
▷ GUIDES *26, 27*

Part I: Write the present participle beside each verb. (Score: 10)

Example:

    live *living* _____

1. begin _____
2. use _____
3. take _____
4. fly _____
5. lie _____

6. see _____
7. drive _____
8. forget _____
9. pay _____
10. stop _____

Part II: Write the past form beside each verb. (Score: 10)

11. plan _____
12. carry _____
13. say _____
14. save _____
15. catch _____

16. match _____
17. fill _____
18. tie _____
19. make _____
20. take _____

Part III: Use each verb in a sentence. (Score: 15—5 for each sentence)

21. (taken) _____

_____

22. (speaking) _____

_____

23. (done) _____

_____

▷ GUIDE *59 WORDSEARCH* (Score: 5) _____

1. drone   larva   queen   pollen
2. bee   spider   bird

Discussion: Include the words in row 1 as you discuss how the animal named in WORDSEARCH builds a home.

45

Name _____ Perfect Score 42   My Score _____

UNIT V/LESSON 42

Recognizing Subject-Verb Agreement

▷ GUIDE 25a, b, d

Part I: Mark through each improper verb. (Score: 12)

Example:

   Kathy Rose (study, studies) the Russian language.
1. She (go, goes) to Russia as often as she can.
2. She (read, reads) Russian newspapers and magazines.
3. Sometimes they (is, are) difficult, but she keeps trying.
4. Kathy (has, have) many Russian friends now.
5. She (meet, meets) people everywhere she goes.
6. Her Russian (is, are) getting better all the time.
7. She always (get, gets) confused on the buses in a new city.
8. Kathy always (speak, speaks) carefully and distinctly so that she will be understood.
9. Russians sometimes (sell, sells) Western goods on the black market.
10. They (pay, pays) a lot for American jeans in Russia.
11. Kathy and the other Americans (try, tries) everything on the menu.
12. They all (agree, agrees) that the dark bread is very good.

Part II: Use each verb below in a sentence. (Score: 30—5 for each sentence)

13. (was) _____

14. (do) _____

15. (does) _____

16. (is) _____

17. (put) _____

18. (left) _____

46

Name _____   Perfect Score 40   My Score ____

UNIT V/LESSON 43

Choosing Subject-Verb Agreement

▷ GUIDE *25a, b, d*

Part I: Mark through each improper verb. (Score: 15)

1. Emily Dickinson (is, are) alive today in her poems.
2. She (speak, speaks) to all who open the pages of her books.
3. From her room in her father's house in Amherst she (listen, listens) to the many secrets of the world.
4. Emily's poems (tell, tells) about simple things.
5. Her love of words (give, gives) order, design, and life to her poems.
6. Emily's own quiet life (reflect, reflects) the values of her New England family.
7. Her poems (reveal, reveals) serenity and self-control.
8. Although she always stayed near home, Emily's range of observation (was, were) wide.
9. No one (know, knows) for sure why Emily lived apart from the world.
10. Do you (think, thinks) that she may have been too sensitive?
11. Perhaps the mere sense of living (is, are) joy enough.
12. People (find, finds) Emily to be an unusual and interesting personality.
13. Her ideas and images (have, has) helped other poets.
14. Mystery and paradox (stare, stares) out of everything near her.
15. With the hymn and the riddle as tools, she (grasp, grasps) at the center of things.

Part II: Write a short paragraph about what you think you would miss if you lived in seclusion. (Score: 25—10 for content, 5 for form, 10 for mechanics)

_____

_____

_____

_____

_____

_____

_____

_____

Name   Perfect Score 39   My Score

UNIT V/LESSON 44

Using Verbs

▷ GUIDES 26, 27

Part I: Underline the verb in each sentence. On the line write the time of the verb action: present, past, or future. (Score: 24)

Example:

    Charlie is enjoying his job as a math teacher.   *present*

1. Charlie teaches math at San Lorenzo High.   _____
2. Perhaps someday he will have his own computer.   _____
3. Right now he is using a hand calculator.   _____
4. Last term he taught students the proper use of the calculator.   _____
5. He was teaching geometry at Aptos High.   _____
6. Most high schools want teachers like Charlie.   _____
7. He makes math exciting for his students.   _____
8. He uses firm discipline with lazy students.   _____
9. Charlie was very tired after this term.   _____
10. He left almost immediately for Guatemala.   _____
11. He imported scarves from Mexico last year.   _____
12. Will he be a millionaire someday?   _____

Part II: Write three sentences. In each sentence use the past tense of the verb in parentheses. (Score: 15—5 for each sentence)

13. (do) _____

_____

14. (draw) _____

_____

15. (drink) _____

_____

Name _____ Perfect Score 52   My Score _____

UNIT V/LESSON 45

Recognizing Verb Tenses

▷ GUIDES 26, 27

Part I: Mark through any verb that does not show action or being in the past. Above the word you marked out, write the form of the verb that expresses past action or being. (Score: 32)

Example:
                        were   *was*
The first stunt fliers ~~are~~ called birdmen, and Lincoln Beachey ~~is~~ the greatest of all.

Before 1908 inventors and airplane builders did their own flying. These are careful and patient people who safely test their own planes and have long careers. After 1908 the birdmen and birdwomen appeared. Daring and reckless, they fly for excitement and prize money at air shows. They flew stunts and tested planes, and many of them die in crashes. Each crash causes the builder to improve that plane.

Lincoln Beachey has a successful career as a show balloonist before he begins flying at 17. In 1906 he becomes famous when he makes the first flight around the Washington Monument. He flew under bridges and over Niagara Falls, and he scoops handkerchiefs off the ground with his wing tip. Always a show-off, he dresses up to fly against Blanche Stuart Scott, a rival flier. He barely avoided a crash, flew loops, and thrills the crowd. He drowns in San Francisco Bay in 1915 when the monoplane he had designed folds in the air during the World's Fair. The Birdman Era ends with his death.

Part II: Use each verb in parentheses to write a sentence. (Score: 15—5 for each sentence)

1. (shall have found) _____

2. (will be making) _____

3. (could have had) _____

▷ GUIDE 59 *WORDSEARCH* (Score: 5) _____
1. paraffin   gasoline   plastic   asphalt
2. iron   hydrogen   petroleum

Discussion: Include the words in row 1 as you discuss the importance of the product named in WORDSEARCH.

Name _____   Perfect Score 30   My Score _____

UNIT V/LESSON 46

Using Active and Passive Voice

▷ GUIDE 24

Part I: Underline the verb in each sentence below. On the line write *active* or *passive* to describe the voice of the verb. (Score: 20—2 for each sentence)

Examples:

Modern cameras <u>can produce</u> color photographs in a few seconds.   *active*

Color photographs <u>can be produced</u> in a few seconds by modern cameras.   *passive*

1. Auguste and Louis Lumière developed the first practical color process in 1907. _____

2. The first practical color process was developed by Auguste and Louis Lumière in 1907. _____

3. The Lumière brothers named this process *autochrome*. _____

4. This process was named *autochrome* by the Lumière brothers. _____

5. Color roll film was introduced in 1935 by Kodak. _____

6. Kodak introduced the color roll film in 1935. _____

7. In 1947 Polaroid introduced the first sixty-second black-and-white photograph. _____

8. In 1947 the first sixty-second black-and-white photograph was introduced by Polaroid. _____

9. The sixty-second color photograph was not produced by Polaroid until 1963. _____

10. Polaroid did not produce the sixty-second color photograph until 1963. _____

Part II: Write each sentence in the active voice. (Score: 10—5 for each sentence)

11. Pleasure can be given by a photograph. _____

_____

12. Views of the world are shown through a camera. _____

_____

Name _____ Perfect Score 29   My Score _____

UNIT V/LESSON 47

Forming Contractions

▷ GUIDE *29*

Part I: Write the contraction for each pair of words. (Score: 10)

1. we will   _____
2. it is   _____
3. will not   _____
4. does not   _____
5. have not   _____

6. they are   _____
7. you are   _____
8. we have   _____
9. who is   _____
10. has not   _____

Part II: In each blank write a contraction that makes sense in the sentence. (Score: 9)

11. American travelers in Russia _____ go wherever they please.

12. Some _____ like this restriction, but _____ a Soviet law.

13. Kathy Rose still _____ really understand Russia.

14. _____ been there eight months working with an American exhibit.

15. In all that time she _____ seen Russia as Russians do.

16. "They _____ let you go any farther than 25 miles from any city."

17. "And you _____ go to some cities at all."

18. _____ there travel restrictions placed on Russian travelers in America, too?

Part III: Write two sentences. In each sentence use the contraction in parentheses. (Score: 10—5 for each sentence)

19. (it's) _____

_____

20. (you're) _____

_____

Name _____   Perfect Score 31   My Score _____

UNIT V/LESSON 48

Choosing Appropriate Forms

▷ GUIDE 26

Part I: In the blank write the appropriate form of the verb in parentheses. (Score: 16)

1. (be)   The $1 bill _____ a piece of paper measuring 2½ by 6 inches.
2. (appear)   The word *dollar* _____ on both sides.
3. (cost)   A batch of notes _____ the government $20.90 to print.
4. (come)   The word *dollar* _____ from the German word *Taler*.
5. (issue)   Before 1861 only coins were _____.
6. (have)   People _____ little faith in paper money during the Colonial period.
7. (decide)   In 1861, Congress _____ to print the first paper currency.
8. (know)   It was _____ as "greenbacks" or "legal tenders."
9. (be)   The dollar, as we know it today, _____ a Federal Reserve note.
10. (issue)   It is _____ by the twelve Federal Reserve banks across the U.S.
11. (guarantee) The Federal Reserve notes are _____ by a pledge of collateral.
12. (coin)   A mint is the place where money is _____ by the government.
13. (supervise) The Secretary of the Treasury _____ the mints.
14. (be)   There _____ now two mints, one in Denver and one in Philadelphia.
15. (wear)   A $1 bill _____ out in about eighteen months.
16. (last)   Bills of higher denomination _____ longer because they are not handled as often.

Part II: Use the verb in parentheses in a sentence. (Score: 15—5 for each sentence)

17. (went) _____

18. (seen) _____

19. (wore) _____

52

Name   Perfect Score 130   My Score

UNIT V/LESSON 49

Using Capitalization and Punctuation

▷ GUIDES *39a–c, e, 45, 48, 52, 53*

Part I: Punctuate the sentences and circle each letter that should be capitalized.
(Score: 80)

1. jamaica is one of the islands in the caribbean sea
2. kingston jamaica has almost the same temperature summer and winter
3. the blue mountains are in the eastern part and heavy rain falls there
4. the hurricane season august to november brings damaging storms
5. christopher columbus landed on the island of jamaica in 1494
6. the arawak indians lived there then but spanish settlers killed most of them
7. the spanish brought in african slaves to work on plantations
8. many europeans chinese and east indians later settled in jamaica
9. the island became a british colony in 1670
10. on august 6 1962 jamaica gained its independence
11. a jamaican artist namba roy became well known in great britain
12. another islander claude mckay came to the united states
13. he wrote such books as harlem shadows and banana bottom

Part II: Write a paragraph. Include the things you found most interesting about Jamaica.
(Score: 25—10 for content, 5 for form, 10 for mechanics)

_____

_____

_____

_____

_____

_____

COMPOSITION: Rewrite your paragraph into an advertisement for a travel magazine.
(Score: 25—10 for content, 5 for form, 10 for mechanics)

Name _____ Perfect Score 27   My Score _____

UNIT V/LESSON 50

Review V

▶ GUIDE 25

Part I: Underline the appropriate word in parentheses. (Score: 5)

1. Three huskies and one poodle (is, are) in the kennel.
2. (Is, Are) there anyone in the house?
3. The Kings (do, does) not live here anymore.
4. You (was, were) supposed to do the dishes.
5. All four of you (is, are) late this morning.

▶ GUIDES 26, 27

Part II: Write the past form beside each verb. (Score: 10)

6. break _____   11. take _____
7. forget _____   12. find _____
8. throw _____   13. lay _____
9. carry _____   14. sit _____
10. stop _____   15. write _____

▶ GUIDE 29

Part III: Write the contraction beside each pair of words. (Score: 12)

16. it is _____   22. I am _____
17. she will _____   23. Casey is _____
18. did not _____   24. has not _____
19. would not _____   25. do not _____
20. will not _____   26. you will _____
21. they are _____   27. have not _____

54

Name _____ Perfect Score 42   My Score _____

UNIT VI/LESSON 51

Recognizing Verbals—Participles

▷ GUIDE *28a, b*

Part I: Find the participles used as adjectives. On the line write the participle and the noun it modifies. (Score: 22)

Example:

    The broken window will be fixed tomorrow. *broken window*

1. Linda drove north in a borrowed car. _____
2. A fallen tree blocked the road. _____
3. Two people with a rented truck removed the tree. _____
4. The car had a dented fender. _____
5. The unplanned delay was a good opportunity for a walk. _____
6. Linda stopped at six for a nicely prepared dinner. _____
7. That night she slept in a room with torn curtains. _____
8. In the morning she drank some poorly brewed coffee. _____
9. The rolling hills looked beautiful to her. _____
10. Congested traffic made her arrive late. _____
11. Her clothes were rumpled and wrinkled. _____

Part II: Put parentheses around each participial phrase. Underline the word it modifies. (Score: 20)

12. Linda rebuilt the radio sitting on the table.
13. She used parts taken from other radios.
14. The tools borrowed from her friend helped a lot.
15. Wires soldered together carry current well.
16. She worked from plans bought at a hardware store.
17. Parts ordered from the East Coast did not arrive for six weeks.
18. The radio now receives programs broadcast from Canada.
19. Linda hopes to get a job repairing small appliances.
20. Yesterday she talked to a person offering office space.
21. Old appliances repaired by a skilled worker are often better than new ones.

55

Name _____ Perfect Score 40   My Score _____

UNIT VI/LESSON 52

Using Participial Phrases

▷ GUIDE *28b*

Part I: Combine two sentences by using a participial phrase. (Score: 20—5 for each sentence)
Example:

The truck was painted in bright colors. It caught Tony's eye.

The truck, painted in bright colors, caught Tony's eye.

1. Tony and his boss were waiting for a bus. They witnessed the accident. _____

2. The truck was taking the turn too fast. It ran into a parked car. _____

3. The car was dented in two places. It would probably still run. _____

4. Police officers arrived at the scene. They took Tony's statement. _____

Part II: Write each sentence so that the participial phrase modifies the appropriate noun. (Score: 20—5 for each sentence)
Example:

Tony saw the accident waiting for a bus.

Waiting for a bus, Tony saw the accident.

5. I saw a new office building walking to the store. _____

6. Jane gave a book to her niece written by Aileen Fisher. _____

7. He hurried out the door paying his check. _____

8. I gave a roast turkey to my sister wrapped in aluminum foil. _____

Name _____   Perfect Score 41   My Score _____

UNIT VI/LESSON 53

Recognizing Verbals—Gerunds

▷ GUIDE *28c*

Part I: Underline each gerund. The gerund may be a subject, a direct object, or a subjective complement. On the line, write the name of the sentence element. (Score: 16)

Examples:

    Diving is an exciting sport.   *subj.*

    Rosalita enjoyed swimming in the ocean.   *dir. obj.*

1. Tumbling is a good way to keep in shape. _____
2. Rosalita stopped her packing at dinner time. _____
3. Waiting makes her nervous. _____
4. Worrying is a waste of time. _____
5. She dislikes discussing her plans. _____
6. Snorkeling bores her. _____
7. Rosalita's greatest joy is snapping pictures of big fish. _____
8. Her job is teaching water safety. _____

Part II: Write five sentences. In each sentence use the verb form in parentheses as a noun. (Score: 25—5 for each sentence)

9. (studying) _____

10. (walking) _____

11. (watching) _____

12. (buying) _____

13. (talking) _____

57

Name _____   Perfect Score 49   My Score _____

UNIT VI/LESSON 54

Using Gerund Phrases

▷ GUIDE *28d*

Part I: Put parentheses around each gerund phrase. Underline the verb. (Score: 14)

Examples:

(Appearing in "Star Trek") made Nichelle Nichols famous. She enjoyed (playing Lt. Uhura in that TV program).

1. Finding new space travelers is Ms. Nichols's job today.
2. She does not mind spending long days on the road.
3. Telling women and members of minority groups about the space shuttle is her job.
4. Talking with Ms. Nichols has interested many people in space travel.
5. Would you enjoy piloting a ship through space?
6. Recruiting for NASA has pleased Nichelle Nichols.
7. She believes in encouraging people toward a space career.

Part II: Write seven sentences. In each sentence use the phrase in parentheses as a noun. (Score: 35—5 for each sentence)

8. (reading the sports page) _____

9. (cooking breakfast) _____

10. (running for a bus) _____

11. (offering her help) _____

12. (eating a hamburger) _____

13. (mailing a postcard) _____

14. (watching television) _____

Name _____ Perfect Score 20   My Score _____

UNIT VI/LESSON 55

Recognizing Verbals—Infinitives

▷ GUIDE *28e*

Part I: Underline the infinitives used as nouns. (Score: 5)

1. To search for lost treasure is exciting.

2. Treasure hunters try to find misers' hoards and pirate loot.

3. To dig up stories from old library files requires patience.

4. Hunters try to recover ancient lanterns, vintage guns, or old coins from abandoned mines.

5. To find a single valuable coin is worth all the effort.

Part II: Underline the infinitives used as adjectives. (Score: 5)

6. Legal rights to hunt treasure vary from state to state.

7. One must have permission to search on private property.

8. One of the largest lost treasures to be found could be near Taos, New Mexico.

9. With enemies to fight, the ancient ruler Montezuma hid more than $10 million.

10. No record to verify that the treasure was ever discovered has been found.

Part III: Underline the infinitives used as adverbs. (Score: 5)

11. In 1876, a young Mexican went to Taos to look for the treasure.

12. He seemed certain to know the treasure's location.

13. Searching among the rocks, he went ahead to outrun the other hunters.

14. Legend says he was heard to call out, "I found it!"

15. Suddenly, he was seen to fall from the cliff, and the site was never revealed.

▷ GUIDE **59** *WORDSEARCH* (Score: 5) _____

1. developer   architect   contractor   realtor
2. retailing   mining   building

Discussion: Include the words in row 1 as you discuss the different occupations found in the industry named by WORDSEARCH.

Name _____   Perfect Score 48   My Score _____

UNIT VI/LESSON 56

Using Infinitive Phrases

▷ GUIDE *28f*

Part I: Put parentheses around each infinitive phrase. (Score: 8)

1. After the tennis tournament, we plan to throw a party.
2. My father hopes to show a video replay of the match.
3. Some guests may prefer to swim.
4. Cecile wants to ask the tennis pro some questions.
5. No one at the party knew how to play a drop shot.
6. The tennis pro told my father to practice more.
7. To win a tournament is exciting!
8. I hope the winners decide to bring their trophies.

Part II: Use each phrase in parentheses in a sentence. (Score: 40—5 for each sentence)

9. (to travel in outer space) _____

10. (to ride a motorcycle) _____

11. (to laugh at a bad joke) _____

12. (to offer your help) _____

13. (to juggle three apples) _____

14. (to rebuild the transmission) _____

15. (to settle an argument) _____

16. (to go to the dentist) _____

Name   Perfect Score 23   My Score

UNIT VI/*LESSON 57*

Choosing Synonyms and Antonyms

Part I: Synonyms are words that have almost the same meaning. Circle the word that has almost the same meaning as the word in italics. (Score: 9)

1. *broad*	narrow	wide	round	expensive
2. *vacant*	occupied	comfortable	empty	apartment
3. *injury*	event	insurance	benefit	hurt
4. *alert*	watchful	dull	earnest	happy
5. *slender*	tall	slim	chance	rotund
6. *save*	keep	earn	safety	bend
7. *caution*	warning	traffic	common	quiet
8. *laws*	police	court	robber	rules
9. *skeleton*	dead	mirage	bones	old

Part II: Antonyms are words that have almost opposite meanings. Circle the word that is most nearly opposite in meaning to the word in italics. (Score: 9)

10. *happy*	sad	laughter	merry	poor
11. *open*	door	empty	close	wide
12. *noisy*	loud	quiet	children	clamor
13. *best*	worst	ugly	perfect	prize
14. *inferior*	pretty	interior	furious	superior
15. *dull*	share	hazy	bright	wax
16. *upper*	lower	teeth	above	basement
17. *rough*	rocky	tough	treatment	smooth
18. *ill*	evil	well	sick	hospital

▷ GUIDE *59 WORDSEARCH* (Score: 5)

1. liter   kilogram   gram   kilometer
2. Roman   Arabic   metric

Discussion: Include the words in row 1 as you discuss the system of measurement named in WORDSEARCH.

Name _____   Perfect Score 29   My Score _____

UNIT VI/LESSON 58

Using Appropriate Forms

▷ GUIDES *26, 27*

Part I: In the blank write the present tense of the verb in parentheses. (Score: 14)

Example:

(buy) Ernie *buys* _____ vitamins he doesn't really need.

1. (carry)   This magazine _____ an advertisement for vitamins.
2. (tell)   Ernie _____ me that he ordered some of these.
3. (look)   Well, Ernie certainly _____ healthy to me.
4. (need)   Is he really sure that he _____ vitamins?
5. (think)   He says that he _____ they won't hurt him.
6. (seem)   It _____ rather foolish to take them for that reason.
7. (say)   The ad _____ that everyone needs them.
8. (see)   A person need not believe all he or she _____ in those ads.
9. (sell)   Besides, the drugstore _____ vitamins.
10. (save)   Don't you _____ money by sending away for them?
11. (charge) No, I'm sure the druggist _____ even less for vitamins.
12. (begin) Now I _____ to wonder whether we've been cheated.
13. (sign)   Now Ernie will think before he _____ another coupon.
14. (hear)   He'll be angry as a hornet when he _____ about this!

Part II: Write three sentences. In each sentence use the verb in parentheses. (Score: 15—5 for each sentence)

15. (is) _____
_____

16. (does) _____
_____

17. (asks) _____
_____

62

Name _____ Perfect Score 60   My Score _____

UNIT VI/LESSON 59

Writing a Paragraph

▷ GUIDE *54a, b*

Use one of the sentences below as the topic sentence of a paragraph. Then write six or more additional sentences that tell about the topic sentence. (Score: 30—10 for content, 5 for form, 15 for mechanics)

Topic Sentences:

There is an amazing person who lives on my street.

Professional sports have become big businesses.

I would rather be somewhere else today.

My family has an interesting history.

I admire one famous person most of all.

COMPOSITION: Clip a short article from a newspaper or a magazine. Underline each participial phrase, gerund phrase, and infinitive phrase. Write the article without using these phrases. (Score: 30—15 for content, 5 for form, 10 for mechanics)

Name _____ Perfect Score 60   My Score _____

UNIT VI/*LESSON 60*

Review VI

▷ GUIDE *28a, b*

Part I: Use each word as an adjective in a sentence. (Score: 15—5 for each sentence)

1. (confused) _____

2. (flying) _____

3. (grown) _____

▷ GUIDE *28b*

Part II: Use each phrase as an adjective in a sentence. (Score: 15—5 for each sentence)

4. (angered by a remark) _____

5. (carried on a platter) _____

6. (singing a song) _____

▷ GUIDE *28c, d*

Part III: Use each phrase as a noun in a sentence. (Score: 15—5 for each sentence)

7. (saving short pieces of string) _____
_____

8. (waiting for a bus) _____
_____

9. (keeping my promise) _____
_____

▷ GUIDE *28e, f*

Part IV: Use each phrase as a noun, an adjective, or an adverb in a sentence. (Score: 15—5 for each sentence)

10. (to stay for dinner) _____
_____

11. (to break old habits) _____

12. (to be happy) _____

64

Name _____ Perfect Score 30   My Score _____

UNIT VII/LESSON 61

Recognizing Dependent Clauses

▷ GUIDE *11a, b*

Part I: Underline the introductory word in each dependent clause. (Score: 10)

Example:

Do you know <u>that</u> water covers seventy percent of the earth?

1. Because we live on land, the ocean seems strange and mysterious.
2. The ocean's beauty attracts us whenever we look out to sea.
3. The ocean scares us, too, because we are not at home there.
4. Although we travel on and under the surface, the ocean is not our home.
5. The ocean is a place where strange and deadly creatures live.
6. Although we have learned a great deal, much remains a mystery.
7. Since the first time we humans went to sea, the shark has frightened us.
8. Sharks are feared and hated because they are known as vicious killers.
9. When we see a fin above the water, we feel a stab of fear.
10. No one enters the water if a shark is swimming nearby.

Part II: Underline the introductory word and put parentheses around each dependent clause. (Score: 20)

Example:

(<u>While</u> most people hate sharks,) their hate is not based on knowledge.

11. If we understood sharks better, we might not be so afraid.
12. While sharks are killers, not all sharks are dangerous to people.
13. Although the whale shark is huge, it is usually harmless.
14. Many other sharks will not attack unless they are aroused.
15. A shark often turns away if it meets a healthy creature its own size.
16. While a shark looks big to us, we also look big to the shark.
17. Many sharks do deserve their reputation, since they often attack people.
18. The tiger, the hammerhead, and the great white are sharks that people must avoid.
19. If we consider size and viciousness, the great white is the most dangerous shark.
20. Although most sharks live in salt water, one dangerous shark lives in fresh water in Lake Nicaragua.

Name _____   Perfect Score 35   My Score _____

UNIT VII/LESSON 62

Writing Complex Sentences

▷ GUIDE *11a, b*

Write a complex sentence by making a dependent clause of one sentence. Use the word in parentheses as the introductory word of the clause. If the dependent clause comes at the beginning of the sentence, put a comma after it. (Score: 35—5 for each sentence)

Example:

Some women have ruled their countries. They were children of kings. (because)
Because they were children of kings, some women have ruled their countries.

1. Some were powerful. Others had no influence on their governments. (although) _____

2. Women have more power in government today. They are elected to important positions. (because) _____

3. Indira Gandhi was elected prime minister of India in 1966. She became the first woman ever elected to head a major government. (when) _____

4. Mrs. Gandhi was defeated in 1977. She was reelected in 1980. (although) _____

5. Israeli Prime Minister Levi Eshkol died in 1969. Golda Meir was appointed to take his place and served until 1974. (when) _____

6. The Conservatives won control of the House of Commons in 1979. Margaret Thatcher became Britain's first female prime minister. (after) _____

7. Women such as these gain experience and respect. More women will be elected to influential positions. (as) _____

Name _____   Perfect Score 50   My Score _____

UNIT VII/LESSON 63

Writing Complex Sentences

▷ GUIDE *11a, b*

Write ten complex sentences. In each sentence use the dependent clause in parentheses. (Score: 50—5 for each sentence)

Examples:

(if I can get tickets) *If I can get tickets, I will go to the game.*

OR: *I will go to the game if I can get tickets.*

1. (although sports events on TV are fine) _____

2. (whenever I can) _____

3. (if you want to join me) _____

4. (unless you tell me by Tuesday) _____

5. (since you can get there quickly) _____

6. (before you start out) _____

7. (because the gates open early) _____

8. (as soon as we arrive) _____

9. (while the game is in progress) _____

10. (after we leave) _____

67

Name _____ Perfect Score 31   My Score _____

UNIT VII/LESSON 64

Recognizing Adjective Clauses

▷ GUIDES *11a, b, 33a*

Part I: An adjective clause is a dependent clause that modifies a noun or pronoun. Put parentheses around each dependent clause and underline the word or words it modifies. (Score: 21)

Example:

    We use many words (that have interesting origins.)

1. A knowledge of word origins helps people who want better vocabularies.
2. Greek and Latin, which are two ancient languages, have given us many words.
3. Do you know the reason why *territory* means "an area of land"?
4. *Terra* is a Latin word that means "land" or "earth."
5. This information can help you at those times when you meet similar words.
6. *Terrain, terrace,* and *terrestrial* are words that come from the same root.
7. Can you tell the meaning that these three words share?
8. We live in an age when people are exploring space.
9. An astronaut is a person whose job is the exploration of space.
10. *Astronaut* comes from two Greek terms that mean "star" and "sailor."

Part II: The words *who, which,* and *that* often introduce adjective clauses. The word *who* refers only to people; *which* refers only to things; *that* may refer to either people or things. Use *who, which,* or *that* to complete each sentence. Remember that a comma never appears before an adjective clause introduced by *that.* (Score: 10)

11. Our word *jet* comes from the French *jeter,* _____ means "to throw."

12. *Jeter* is a verb _____ comes from the Latin verb *jacere.*

13. Many English words have the root *ject,* _____ is added to a prefix.

14. A player _____ is ejected from a game is "thrown out" of the game.

15. Have you ever been rejected for a job _____ required more experience?

16. "I object!" is a term _____ is often heard during a trial.

17. What words besides *dejected* would describe people _____ are downcast?

18. A jetty is a structure _____ extends into the water to protect a harbor.

19. Smoking is a habit _____ has become objectionable to many.

20. A singer _____ can project his or her voice may not need a microphone.

68

Name _____ Perfect Score 26   My Score _____

UNIT VII/LESSON 65

Recognizing Adverb Clauses

▷ GUIDES *11a, b, 34a–c*

Part I: An adverb clause is a dependent clause that modifies a verb, an adjective, an adverb, or the whole main clause. Put a comma after each adverb clause that comes at the beginning of a sentence. Underline each adverb clause that does not. (Score: 16)

Examples:

I made my plans <u>before my vacation began</u>.

Because it was so cold up north, I decided on a trip south.

1. Although I had visited South America I had never been to Mexico.
2. While we were flying over Texas we passed through a storm.
3. After our plane landed in Mexico City we checked into our hotel.
4. When we finished unpacking we took a long walk.
5. We were often short of breath because the city is at a high altitude.
6. Since Mexico City has many fine restaurants we dined very well.
7. After we had lunch we took a short nap.
8. After a short drive through the city we headed for Taxco and Acapulco.
9. As we drove a huge snowcapped volcano came into view.
10. We were quite awed when we saw Popocatepetl, the famous peak.
11. Although it was close it seemed faraway.
12. We could see the peak clearly because the day was so bright and sunny.
13. We followed the main road until we reached the Taxco turnoff.
14. After we spent a week enjoying Mexico City's activity Taxco was a pleasant change.
15. We spent several hours on the beach at Acapulco because the weather was so beautiful.
16. When you spend a week in Acapulco you return home with a better outlook on life.

Part II: Write two sentences. In each sentence use the word in parentheses as the introductory word of a dependent clause. (Score: 10—5 for each sentence)

17. (when) _____

_____

18. (although) _____

_____

Name _____ Perfect Score 60   My Score _____

UNIT VII/LESSON 66

Combining Sentences

▷ GUIDES *9, 10, 11a–b*

First write a compound sentence by combining the two short sentences with *or, and,* or *but*. Then write a complex sentence by making a dependent clause of one sentence. Notice how different dependent clauses change the meaning. (Score: 60—5 for each sentence)

Examples:

Anne was a well-known writer. She was young.

Anne was a well-known writer, and she was young.

Anne was a well-known writer when she was young.

Although she was young, Anne was a well-known writer.

1. Anne studied literature at a community college. She worked for a publisher.

2. She was still in school. Two of her stories were published.

3. Anne graduated with honors. She wrote for magazines.

4. She sold many fine stories. Her first story was rejected.

5. She worked hard. Her stories were successful.

6. Anne wrote a very fine story. She expanded it into a novel.

Name _____   Perfect Score 50   My Score _____

UNIT VII/LESSON 67

Choosing Appropriate Forms

▷ GUIDES *15a–d, 22–27*

Write sentences using each word in parentheses. (Score: 45—5 for each sentence)

Example: (our) *Did you like our story about the shark?*

1. (your) _____

2. (you're) _____

3. (its) _____

4. (it's) _____

5. (their) _____

6. (they're) _____

7. (see) _____

8. (hear) _____

9. (taste) _____

▷ GUIDE *59 WORDSEARCH* (Score: 5) _____

1. egg larva pupa adult
2. whitefish wasp robin

Discussion: Include the words in row 1 as you discuss the life cycle of the animal named in WORDSEARCH.

71

Name _____ Perfect Score 50   My Score _____

UNIT VII/LESSON 68

Revising a Paragraph

▷ GUIDES *15a, 29–31, 34d, 35, 57a*

Draw a line through any misspelled word in the paragraph and write the correct spelling above it. Use a dictionary to help you. [(Score: 45)]

Example: Scott Joplin ~~wuz~~ *was* born in ~~Texus~~ *Texas* 1868.

Scott Joplin was one of the grate musicians and composers in our histry. When he was foreteen years old, he headed fore Missouri. He plaid the piano their and on riverbouts. He was good at playing a new kind of music. This music had a funy and triky beet, so it was calld "ragged time" music, or "ragtime." Latar, his freinds urged him to studi music. He becam a composer, useing the style of ragtime music to rite everthing from ballets to operas. His poplar music, calld "rags," was veri wel known. The "Maple Leaf Rag" is specialy famus. However, no won was intrested in Joplin's serius music. Peepul wood lissen to him play but were not willing to giv him credit as a riter of serious music. He continud to work hard, tho his operas fayled. His most ambiscious work was the opera "Treemonisha." He put all his mony into a preformance of it. It was a desaster that destroid him. He dyed in a hospital in 1917. He is considered a uinque composer, and he is lovd and admird threwout the world.

▷ GUIDE *59* **WORDSEARCH** (Score: 5) _____

1. retina pupil lens iris
2. eye flower camera

Discussion: Include the words in row 1 as you discuss the parts and operation of the structure named in WORDSEARCH.

72

Name _____   Perfect Score 55   My Score _____

UNIT VII/*LESSON 69*

Writing a Paragraph

▷ GUIDE *54*

Write a descriptive or informative paragraph of eight or more sentences. Use an original subject or one of those below. Before you write, plan the order in which you will tell your ideas. It may help you to write some notes on another sheet of paper first. (Score: 25—10 for content, 5 for form, 10 for mechanics)

Titles:

    A Person I Will Always Remember   Tuning an Automobile Engine

    An Important Event in My Life   A Perfect Dinner

    An Unforgettable Sight   What I Expect in a Friend

_____

_____

_____

_____

_____

_____

_____

_____

_____

_____

_____

_____

_____

_____

_____

COMPOSITION: Write a paragraph explaining to a friend how to make a salad. Underline each dependent clause you use. (Score: 30—10 for content, 10 for form, 10 for mechanics)

Name _____ Perfect Score 55   My Score _____

UNIT VII/*LESSON 70*

Review VII

▷ GUIDE *11a, b*

Write eleven complex sentences. In each sentence use the clause in parentheses. (Score: 55—5 for each sentence)

1. (that I saw on the fire escape) _____

2. (which happened so suddenly) _____

3. (who owns the delicatessen) _____

4. (that I found in my soup) _____

5. (that she was a carpenter) _____

6. (when he stepped on the skateboard) _____

7. (although this sounds silly) _____

8. (if you know the story already) _____

9. (while we're on the subject) _____

10. (where people go barefoot) _____

11. (that she gave) _____

74

Name _____   Perfect Score 47   My Score _____

UNIT VII/LESSON 71

Writing a Business Letter

▷ GUIDES *55a, b, 56*

Write the following business letter. Arrange the parts properly. Use appropriate capitalization and punctuation. (Score: 42)

109 hales drive springfield missouri 65811 february 16 1983 product manager for batteries speedy flash products inc 725 princeton ave des moines iowa 50309 dear product manager two months ago i put three speedy flash batteries into my flashlight these batteries have corroded and cannot be removed since you guarantee to replace any flashlight damaged by your batteries i am sending my flashlight to you for replacement yours truly dana hobbie

▷ GUIDE *59 WORDSEARCH* (score: 5)

1. Seine River   franc   Paris   Riviera
2. Portugal   France   Germany

Discussion: Include the words in row 1 as you discuss the exports of the country named in WORDSEARCH.

75

Name _____ Perfect Score 50   My Score ___

UNIT VIII/LESSON 72

Writing a Business Letter

▷ GUIDES *55a, b, 56*

Write a letter to Dr. May Tate, Hill's Veterinary Hospital, 585 Cicero Street, Arlington Heights, Illinois 60006. Ask for information on how to care for a puppy. Address the envelope. (Score: 50—15 for content, 20 for form, 15 for mechanics)

Name   Perfect Score 50   My Score

UNIT VIII/*LESSON 73*

Writing a Business Letter

▷ GUIDES *55a, b, 56*

Write a letter and address the envelope to the Customer Relations Manager of Tidewater Cleaners, Box 341, Baltimore, Maryland 21220. Explain that the company's local shop lost two of your garments. Describe the garments, tell their value, and ask the company to repay you. (Score: 50—15 for content, 20 for form, 15 for mechanics)

Name _____   Perfect Score 33   My Score _____

UNIT VIII/LESSON 74

Completing an Application Form

▷ GUIDE 58

In each blank write the information requested.

CUSTOMER SERVICE APPLICATION

Date _____   Do Not Write in This Space

Telephone _____

Name _____
        Last   First   Middle

Address _____
         Street   City   State

How long have you lived at this address? _____

Do you own your home? _____ Rent? _____ House _____ Apt. _____

Do you own a car? _____ Are you presently paying for a car? _____

Do you have a bank account? _____ Savings _____ Checking _____

Name of bank _____ Address of bank _____

List companies where you presently have charge accounts.

1. _____
    Company   Address   Telephone

2. _____
    Company   Address   Telephone

List three persons (not relatives) who have known you for five years or more.

1. _____
    Name   Address   Telephone

2. _____
    Name   Address   Telephone

3. _____
    Name   Address   Telephone

Your Signature _____

Name _____ Perfect Score 13   My Score _____

UNIT VIII/LESSON 75

Completing an Employment Test

▷ GUIDE *58*

When you apply for a job, you are often given some tests. Your answers to such tests may show how carefully you read, how well you understand instructions, and whether you follow directions. With this in mind, read carefully and answer as directed.

1. Mark through every word in the next line that does not rhyme with *might*.

   kite   thought   night   knight   length   height

2. Smoking in a service station may not be permitted because (check one)

   (a) it looks as if you are not working. _____

smoking near gasoline is dangerous. _____ (b)

it makes stains on your fingers. _____ (c)

3. Read the paragraph (b). Fill each blank with a word from the list (a) that makes sense in the sentence. Use each word only once.

   (a) don't   country   birds   cats   city   dogs

   (b) Robins are _____ that live in both the _____ and the country.

   In the city, _____ may attack robins. In the _____, robins may

   have other enemies. Cats move much faster than _____. Perhaps that is

   why dogs _____ worry birds very much.

4. Read the paragraph. Then mark the answers below the paragraph.
   Electric cars may be very popular in a few years. They are quiet and cheap to operate, and they do not pollute the air with gases. Only a few electric cars are now in operation. No one has yet invented a satisfactory battery for the electric car. The best of today's electric cars must recharge their batteries every hundred miles or so.

   (a) This paragraph is about traffic control.   true _____ false _____

   (b) Electric cars are not very noisy.   true _____ false _____

   (c) Few people drive electric cars.   true _____ false _____

5. Read the following information. Then circle the answer.

   You work in a restaurant. A customer wishes to pay for her order. The total cost is $2.46. The customer gives you a five-dollar bill. What is the correct change?

   (a) two one-dollar bills, one quarter, two dimes, four pennies
   (b) two one-dollar bills, two quarters, four pennies

Name _____   Perfect Score 25   My Score _____

UNIT VIII/LESSON 76

Finding Information

All the information necessary to complete the statements below can be found in the *Guides*, which begin on page 98. Look through the guides to find the information. Then fill each blank to complete the statement.

1. The conjunctions *and*, *but*, and *or* are commonly used to join the parts of a _____ sentence.

2. Predicate nouns and predicate adjectives are _____ _____.

3. A complex sentence contains a _____ clause and a _____ clause.

4. The _____ principal part of a verb is never used with a helping verb.

5. A _____ clause depends on the rest of the sentence for its meaning.

6. _____, _____, and _____ are three of the pronouns that may be used as direct or indirect objects.

7. A participle is a _____ that can be used as an _____.

8. To express a command you will probably use an _____ sentence.

9. Both the _____ and the _____ of a simple sentence may be compound.

10. A singular verb should not be used with a plural subject, since the _____ must agree with the _____.

11. A transitive verb must have an _____ to express a complete action.

12. The present participle of every verb ends with the suffix _____.

13. The word to which a pronoun refers is its _____.

14. A group of words without a subject-verb relationship cannot be a _____.

15. A word such as *who*, *that*, or *because* often introduces a _____ _____.

16. A prepositional phrase may be used as an _____ or _____.

17. *Of*, *from*, and *with* are _____.

80

Name _____   Perfect Score 55   My Score _____

UNIT VIII/LESSON 77

Writing a Paragraph

▷ GUIDE *54a, b*

Choose one of the activities below. Think carefully before you begin writing. (Score: 50—20 for content, 10 for form, 20 for mechanics)

(a) Write one or more paragraphs explaining to a friend how he or she should go about finding a job.

(b) Write one or more paragraphs telling a friend how he or she should decide what to study in college or junior college.

▷ GUIDE *59 WORDSEARCH* (Score: 5)

1. idea   patent   production   sales
2. injection   invention   ignition

Discussion: Include the words in row 1 as you discuss the process named in WORDSEARCH.

Name _____ Perfect Score 34   My Score _____

UNIT VIII/LESSON 78

Choosing Appropriate Forms

▷ GUIDES *31, 32*

Part I: Mark through each inappropriate form. (Score: 19)

It was summer in the tropics. Six fat clouds (lay, laid) lazily about the baby blue sky. Two figures in white (sat, set) in the shade of a tattered green awning. Before them (laid, lay) a jetsam-covered beach and the blue Pacific.

"Then, are we all (sat, set) for tomorrow morning?" asked the shell collector. He slowly and dramatically (lay, laid) his open hand on the table top.

"It's all been (laid, lay) out as you asked," said the trader, showing no emotion. "The boat arrangements are now (set, sat). The diver is (sitting, setting) in the hotel waiting for instructions. Tomorrow afternoon you should be (setting, sitting) aboard the flight to Auckland. And the treasure should be (laying, lying) safely in your flight bag."

"Good," said the collector. Five $1000 bills were (lay, laid) on the table. There would be five more for the trader if all went as planned. The treasure at that moment (lay, laid) somewhere out in the Pacific. It was calmly poisoning its dinner. The collector had (set, sat) his mind on coming away with the largest specimen of Glory-of-the-Seas ever sighted. Nowadays only a few of these cones (lay, lie) on the ocean floor. Prized by collectors, these creatures have shells of overwhelming beauty.

But the biggest mistake one can make is to greedily pick up a Glory-of-the-Seas (laying, lying) on the sandy bottom. It will send its tiny harpoon into your skin. You'll (sit, set) down. Then you'll (lay, lie) down. And you'll probably never get up.

Not all the danger (lays, lies) in the catching of this deadly beauty. The collector knew this only too well. He (lay, laid) awake all night on the hammock, thinking through the plan again and again and again.

Part II: Write sentences using the verbs in parentheses. (Score: 15—5 for each sentence)

1. (sit) _____

_____

2. (sat) _____

_____

3. (set) _____

_____

Name _____   Perfect Score 66   My Score _____

UNIT VIII/LESSON 79

Using a Dictionary—Word Division

▷ GUIDE *57a–c*

It is often necessary to divide a word at the end of a line of writing. Typists, particularly, must be skilled at proper word division. Each entry word in a dictionary shows where a word may be divided. For speed in finding the words listed below, first list them in alphabetical order. Then show their syllables according to the entry words in your dictionary. Use a hyphen between syllables. (Score: 36)

Example:

recriminate   *re-crim-i-nate*

deposit	1.		
order	2.		
thought	3.		
accept	4.		
rather	5.		
razor	6.		
envelope	7.		
hundred	8.		
really	9.		
quiet	10.		
niece	11.		
appointment	12.		
dependable	13.		
driving	14.		
stopper	15.		
invoice	16.		
application	17.		
garage	18.		

COMPOSITION: Write a paragraph explaining to a friend the importance of the form of a business letter. (Score: 30—10 for contents, 10 for form, 10 for mechanics)

83

Name _____   Perfect Score 50   My Score _____

UNIT VIII/LESSON 80

Review VIII

▷ GUIDES *55a, b, 56*

Write a short business letter asking for information about a product; then address the envelope. You may use the name and address of an actual business firm, or you may make up a name and address. (Score: 50—15 for content, 20 for form, 15 for mechanics)

Name _____   Perfect Score 44   My Score _____

UNIT IX/LESSON 81

Reviewing Sentences

▷ GUIDES *9, 10, 11a, b*

Part I: Punctuate each sentence. On the line tell whether the sentence is simple, compound, or complex. (Score: 29)

1. The great whales and dolphins are mammals _____
2. They breathe air and the females nurse their young with milk _____
3. When they want to breathe they must go to the surface _____
4. The blue whale is the world's biggest animal _____
5. Dolphins and porpoises look similar but they are different _____
6. The dolphin's greater size and intelligence set it apart _____
7. Cetaceans often swim together and communicate with each other _____
8. When a dolphin gets sick another dolphin helps it _____
9. The sick dolphin rests and the "nurse" helps it to the surface _____
10. Female cetaceans often help another female when a calf is born _____
11. Many dolphins and whales have large and complex brains _____
12. Scientists are studying dolphin communication _____

Part II: Write a simple, a compound, and a complex sentence. (Score: 15—5 for each sentence)

13. _____

14. _____

15. _____

Name _____ Perfect Score 40   My Score _____

UNIT IX/*LESSON 82*

Reviewing Sentence Elements

▷ GUIDES *3–6, 9, 33a, b*

There are two important elements in a sentence: the subject and the verb. Everything else in the sentence relates to these elements. A diagram can help you understand how the elements are related. Look at this simple sentence: **John ran.**

A. Draw a straight line and divide it into two equal parts representing the two parts of a sentence.

On the left side of the sentence line write the subject. On the right side write the verb.

Diagram this sentence: **Rain fell.**
(Score: 6—3 for each word)

(Subject)	(Verb)
John	ran

1. _____|_____

The direct object in a sentence tells who or what received the action of the verb. In the sentence **Kelly played ball, Kelly** is the subject, **played** is the verb, and **ball** is the direct object.

B. The subject and the verb are diagramed the same way as in part A. The direct object is related to both the subject and the verb. It is written on the verb side of the line and separated from the verb by a short line.

Diagram this sentence: **Luis likes music.**
(Score: 9—3 for each word)

(Subject)	(Verb)	(Direct Object)
Kelly	played	ball

2. _____|_____|_____

Adjectives modify nouns and pronouns. They answer the questions, "Which one? What kind? How many?" In the sentence **Three small children sang, children** is the subject, **sang** is the verb, and **Three** and **small** are adjectives.

C. The subject and the verb are diagramed the same way as in part A. The adjectives modify the subject and are written on a line under the word they modify.

Diagram this sentence: **Four blue birds ate small seeds.**
(Score: 15—3 for each word)

(Subject)	(Verb)
(Adjective)	
children	sang
small	
Three	

3.

On a separate sheet of paper, diagram the following sentences. (Score: 10—5 for each sentence)

4. Grasshoppers eat green leaves.

5. My brother won the first contest.

Name _____ Perfect Score 39   My Score _____

UNIT IX/LESSON 83

Reviewing Verbals

▷ GUIDE *28a–f*

Part I: Underline the verbal or verbal phrase in each sentence. On the line name the kind of verbal underlined: participle, gerund, or infinitive. (Score: 24)

1. Louis Armstrong learned to play the trumpet as a young boy. _____
2. He soon became the leader of a small marching band. _____
3. Playing trumpet got him a job on a riverboat. _____
4. The job helped his music-reading skill. _____
5. In 1924 Louis decided to marry Lillian Hardin. _____
6. Soon record producers gave him recording sessions. _____
7. By 1926 his trumpeting was famous throughout the United States. _____
8. Visiting many countries brought him fame. _____
9. He was able to introduce American jazz to Europeans. _____
10. He was a featured performer in several movies. _____
11. Louis Armstrong loved entertaining. _____
12. People loved his playing. _____

Part II: Write a sentence using the word in parentheses as an adjective. (Score: 5)

13. (arguing) _____

Part III: Write a sentence using the phrase in parentheses as an adverb. (Score: 5)

14. (to tell the truth) _____

Part IV: Write a sentence using the phrase in parentheses as a noun. (Score: 5)

15. (craning my neck) _____

87

Name _____ Perfect Score 27   My Score _____

UNIT IX/LESSON 84

Reviewing Dependent Clauses

▷ GUIDES *11a, b, 21, 37a*

Part I: Underline the dependent clause in each sentence. On the line tell whether it is used as an adjective or as an adverb. (Score: 10)

1. Loch Ness is a lake that reportedly has a monster. _____

2. Because people love monster tales, this lake has become famous. _____

3. Many who are fascinated by the legend have visited Loch Ness. _____

4. Loch Ness, which is very deep, has not been fully explored. _____

5. When clear pictures are finally taken, the legend may become fact. _____

Part II: Combine each pair of sentences by making a dependent adverbial clause of one sentence. Use the subordinating conjunction in parentheses. (Score: 12—3 for each sentence)

6. Some people believe in the monster. They are fascinated by strange things.   (because)

   _____
   _____

7. I've never seen a clear picture of it. I don't believe in the monster.   (since)

   _____
   _____

8. I was in Scotland. I stopped at Loch Ness to look for the monster.   (while)

   _____
   _____

9. I saw the thick fog. I didn't realize the foolishness of my plan.   (until)

   _____
   _____

▷ GUIDE *59 WORDSEARCH* (Score: 5) _____

1. plate   bifocal   tempered   obsidian
2. metal   china   glass

Discussion: Include the words in row 1 as you discuss products that are made from the substance named in WORDSEARCH.

Name _____   Perfect Score 23   My Score _____

UNIT IX/LESSON 85

Reveiwing Verbs and Adverbs

▷ GUIDES 5, 25a–d, 34a–d

Part I: Mark through the verb that does not agree with the subject. (Score: 14)

1. Birds (show, shows) signs of being related to reptiles.
2. Both birds and reptiles (lay, lays) eggs.
3. According to many scientists, feathers (represent, represents) the remains of scales.
4. A bird (grow, grows) new feathers as old ones wear out.
5. The old feathers (fall, falls) out in a regular pattern.
6. This (is, are) a process called moulting.
7. Birds (have, has) a constant body temperature.
8. The bones in a bird's skeleton (is, are) basically hollow and quite light.
9. However, the heart of a bird (is, are) rather heavy.
10. A bird's heart (beat, beats) four to ten times as fast as the human heart.
11. Powerful breast muscles (provide, provides) strength for flight.
12. The pages of my book (list, lists) more than eight thousand species of birds.
13. Birdwatchers (identify, identifies) two or three new species each year.
14. A birdwatcher (do, does) not need special training.

Part II: An adverb is shown on a diagram the same way as an adjective: on a straight line under the word it modifies. Diagram the sentences below. (Score: 9—1 for each word)

15. Most birds fly swiftly.

16. Many birdwatchers count birds daily.

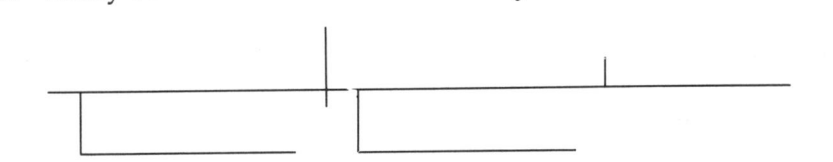

Name _____   Perfect Score 27   My Score _____

UNIT IX/LESSON 86

Reviewing Compound Elements

▷ GUIDES 4–9, 37c

Part I: Write a sentence. Use the element in parentheses. (Score: 10—2 for each sentence)

1. (a noun and pronoun as a compound subject) _____

2. (a compound verb) _____

3. (a compound direct object) _____

4. (two adjectives as a compound subjective complement) _____

5. (two nouns as a compound subjective complement) _____

Part II: To diagram a compound element use a double line. Diagram the following sentences on the lines below. (Score: 17)

6. Tin cans and glass jars preserve food and beverages well.

7. We washed and dried our large jars.

Name _____   Perfect Score 55   My Score _____

UNIT IX/*LESSON 87*

Reviewing Parts of Speech

▷ GUIDES *12–14, 22–28, 33a, b, 34a–c*

Write sentences using each italicized word as indicated. (Score: 55—5 for each sentence)

1. (*rules* as a noun) _____

2. (*rules* as a verb) _____

3. (*back* as a noun) _____

4. (*back* as a verb) _____

5. (*back* as an adverb) _____

6. (*spring* as a noun) _____

7. (*spring* as a verb) _____

8. (*spring* as an adjective) _____

9. (*well* as a noun) _____

10. (*well* as an adverb) _____

11. (*fine* as a noun) _____

91

Name _____ Perfect Score 23   My Score _____

UNIT IX/LESSON 88

Reviewing Appropriate Forms

▷ GUIDES *15, 26, 27, 29–31, 33, 34*

Choose the appropriate form in parentheses and write it in the blank. (Score: 18)

1. (don't, doesn't)   Paula _____ want to talk to her cousin, Joe Superstar.
2. (real, very)   Joe can probably give Paula some _____ good advice.
3. (any, no)   She won't get better suggestions from _____ other star.
4. (took, taken)   Finally she swallowed her pride and _____ the train.
5. (did, done)   That was certainly the smartest thing she ever _____.
6. (saw, seen)   Joe _____ right away that Paula was a good singer.
7. (them, those)   He sent her to one of _____ Rockout Hall auditions.
8. (sat, set)   She was scared when she _____ there waiting to go on.
9. (teach, learn)   The experience did _____ her how to do auditions.
10. (your, you're)   If _____ well trained, it's easy to perform for strangers.
11. (in, into)   Paula passed the audition and went _____ the music business.
12. (its, it's)   She soon learned that rock 'n' roll has _____ good and bad points.
13. (good, well)   Her agent told her that she was progressing _____.
14. (gave, given)   She was _____ all the concerts she could do.
15. (she, her)   Fans have written letters to the band and _____.
16. (ever, never)   But Wendy hardly _____ writes letters.
17. (one, won)   She was _____ of the best friends Paula had.
18. (its, it's)   But _____ hard to convince someone to write a letter.

▷ GUIDE *59 WORDSEARCH* (Score: 5) _____

1. spine folio copyright binding
2. ski book skeleton

Discussion: Include the words in row 1 as you discuss how the item in WORDSEARCH is produced.

Name _____   Perfect Score 84   My Score _____

UNIT IX/LESSON 89

Reviewing Capitalization and Punctuation

▷ GUIDES *39–43, 45, 46, 48, 55*

Arrange, capitalize, and punctuate the following letter. (Score: 59)

916 north aspen street cumberland indiana 46229 july 19 1985 mrs alice webb webb and skogsted insurance brokers 100 sunrise boulevard fort wayne indiana 46800 dear mrs webb on june 6 1985 i wrote you asking how to purchase medical insurance you sent me a pamphlet entitled protection and peace of mind you also wrote that you would call me soon to arrange a meeting i have heard nothing since then and i have been unable to reach you by phone if i dont hear from you by thursday july 24 i will go elsewhere for my insurance sincerely felipe alvarez

COMPOSITION: Write two paragraphs describing the most useful information you found in this book and the ways in which it was helpful. (Score: 25—10 for content, 5 for form, 10 for mechanics)

Name _____   Perfect Score 169   My Score _____

UNIT IX/LESSON 90

Review IX

▷ GUIDES 15, 26, 27, 29, 32

Part I: Underline the appropriate word in parentheses. (Score: 11)

1. Jamie (set, sat) the timer and (lay, laid) down in the sun.
2. The band has (gone, went) to the Cotton Bowl twice.
3. Take this saw to that woman over (their, there).
4. (Who's, Whose) interested in hearing Jane Fonda speak?
5. My fingers are (froze, frozen) stiff.
6. You may split the reward (between, among) the four of you.
7. (They're, There, Their) are going to be over 15,000 people at the game.
8. I wish someone would (learn, teach) me how to drive.
9. The clowns (is, are) leading the parade.
10. Both of (us, we) girls are in the school play.

Write a sentence using the word in parentheses. (Score 10—5 for each sentence)

11. (you're) _____

12. (done) _____

▷ GUIDES 3–6, 9, 33a, b, 34a, d

Part II: Diagram the following sentences. (Score: 18)

13. A large, brown dog ate my sandwich.

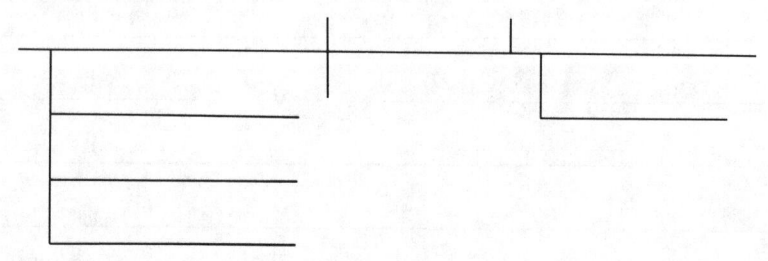

14. Terry ran the race slowly.

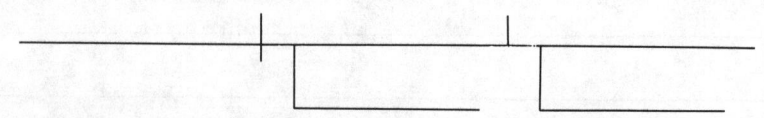

15. Michael and Pat left school early.

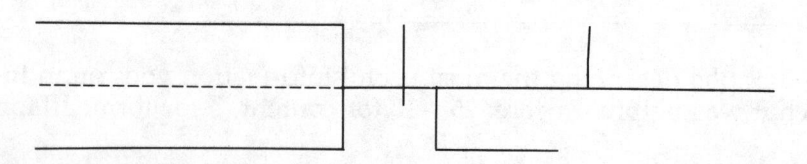

94

▷ GUIDE **28**

Part III: Underline the verbal or verbals in each sentence. On the line write the type of verbal or verbals: *participle, gerund,* or *infinitive.* (Score: 16)

16. Barbara likes to play basketball. _____

17. I found a book printed in 1865. _____

18. Is there any way to save the plants? _____

19. We are ready to begin the race. _____

20. Decaying leaves are a good mulch. _____

21. We talked about hunting and fishing. _____

22. We'll be ready to go this afternoon. _____

Write sentences using the italicized words as indicated. (Score 15—5 for each sentence)

23. (*checked* as an adjective) _____

24. (*screaming* as a subject) _____

25. (*to lock the door* as a noun) _____

▷ GUIDE **36a, b**

Part IV: Circle each preposition. Underline each prepositional phrase. (Score: 18)

26. The box is under the bed in the middle bedroom.

27. Cover the cake with plastic wrap and put it on the table.

28. Raisins are between aisles eight and nine on a display rack.

29. We plan to leave for Miami near the first of July.

Part V: Underline each pronoun. Above each pronoun write how it is used in the sentence: *S* for subject, *DO* for direct object, *IO* for indirect object, and *OP* for object of a preposition. (Score: 18)

30. Tami and I are going to the movies with them.

31. She gave him the present.

32. Dad brought us pizza for dinner.

33. He left it in the oven.

34. They lent the lawn mower to her.

▷ GUIDES *9–11, 21, 37*

Part VI: On the line write the type of sentence: *simple, compound,* or *complex.* If a sentence is compound, circle the conjunction. If the sentence is complex, underline the dependent clause. (Score: 16)

35. I'll get the car while you check out. _____

36. Do you have enough money? _____

37. Carol gave me three dollars, and Celia gave me five dollars. _____

38. After we finish here, we need to go to the bakery. _____

39. Lindy is going to be surprised. _____

40. Since we forgot her birthday last year, she expects us to forget it again. _____

41. I dropped a carton of ice cream, but it didn't break. _____

42. After we eat dinner, we can go to the movies. _____

43. There are several new ones in town. _____

44. Lindy likes scary movies best. _____

▷ GUIDES *2, 39–41, 51, 52*

Part VII: Add all the necessary punctuation to the paragraph below. Underline any letter that should be capitalized. (Score: 47)

its hard to imagine a time without stereos hamburgers zippers and paper cups but theres a first time for everything did you know that leonardo da vinci designed the first contact lenses in 1508 these lenses were to fit over the white part of the eye the first lenses were not made however until 1887 and they were quite uncomfortable if you had lived in the seventeenth century and were hard of hearing you could have used an ear trumpet the ear trumpet was a long horn you put the small end in your ear and the large end toward the sound alexander graham bell invented the first electronic hearing aid in 1876 the chinese used ice cellars more than three thousand years ago but it wasnt until late in the nineteenth century that we had our first home refrigerator the modern safety razor with a disposable blade was first sold by k c gillette in 1903 and col jacob schick patented the first electric shaver in 1923

GUIDES

The guide numbers on the lesson pages direct you to the information given in the following pages. There are fifty-nine guides, many of which are divided into parts. The guides present rules, explanations, examples, and practice exercises.

It is helpful to form the habit of using the guides in this section of this book whenever you need to review language rules or find information about language problems. The guides are indexed in alphabetical order at the end of this book.

THE SENTENCE

▷ GUIDE **1a A sentence expresses a complete thought.**

A sentence must have a subject-verb relationship. The subject is the person, thing, or idea that the sentence is about. The verb expresses the action or state of being of the subject.

He left.

He	left
(subject)	(verb)

1b A group of words without a subject-verb relationship is not a sentence.

men in the factory

men	(verb?)

is running fast

(subject?)	is running

Practice: Check each group of words that is a sentence.

_____ 1. Foggy all morning   _____ 4. Will you call a taxi

_____ 2. She is on this flight   _____ 5. However, I arrived early

_____ 3. Didn't get the luggage   _____ 6. By that time

Kinds of Sentences

▷ GUIDE **2a A declarative sentence, or statement, is a sentence that tells something.**

Put a period after a declarative sentence.

The rain froze on the steps.

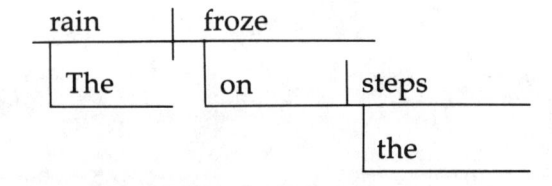

rain	froze
The	on	steps
		the

Practice: Punctuate each declarative sentence.
1. Elena said nothing   2. It is ten o'clock   3. Ching-Wei sent me this postcard

2b An interrogative sentence, or question, is a sentence that asks something.

Put a question mark after an interrogative sentence.

Did the rain freeze on the steps?

rain	Did freeze
the	on	steps
		the

Practice: Punctuate each interrogative sentence.
1. Can you explain this   2. Can't he tell me   3. Won't Jill be able to sing

2c An imperative sentence is a sentence that expresses a request or command.

The subject of an imperative sentence is *you*, although it my not appear in the sentence. Put a period after an imperative sentence.

Be careful on the icy steps.

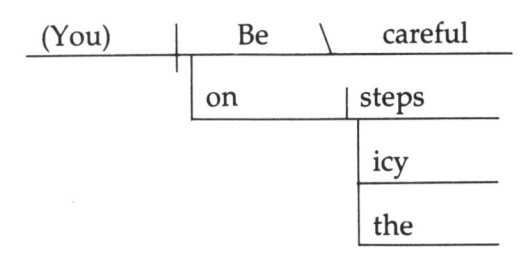

Practice: Punctuate each imperative sentence.
1. Show him how to wrap that package for mailing
2. Please repair that lamp in the hall closet
3. Read Erma Bombeck's column to me

2d An exclamatory sentence is a sentence that expresses strong or sudden feeling.

Put an exclamation point after an exclamatory sentence.

How slippery the steps are!

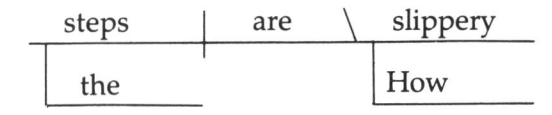

Practice: Punctuate each exclamatory sentence.
1. How beautiful the light looks through that stained glass
2. What a stupid remark for anyone to make
3. Why, it's Millie Perkins from my hometown

Answers to Practice Exercises, Pages 98 and 99

Guides 1a, b
1. She is on this flight   4. Will you call a taxi   5. However, I arrived early

Guide 2a
1. Elena said nothing.   2. It is ten o'clock.   3. Ching-Wei sent me this postcard.

Guide 2b
1. Can you explain this?   2. Can't he tell me?   3. Won't Jill be able to sing?

Guide 2c
1. Show him how to wrap that package for mailing.
2. Please repair that lamp in the hall closet.
3. Read Erma Bombeck's column to me.

Guide 2d
1. How beautiful the light looks through that stained glass!
2. What a stupid remark for anyone to make!
3. Why, it's Millie Perkins from my hometown!

Correct any mistakes.

SENTENCE ELEMENTS

▷ GUIDE 3 The natural order of the main elements in a sentence is usually the following: subject, verb, object or subjective complement.

Sentence elements sometimes appear in another order.

The shoes are muddy.

That question he did not ask.

Practice: Write the following sentences in natural order.
1. From upstairs came the clack of a typewriter.

2. This new book of science fiction you just must read.

Subject

▷ GUIDE 4 The subject of a sentence is the word that names the person, thing, or idea about which something is being said.

The *sky* glows.   *Isaac* mailed the letter.   Had *she* written it?

The subject may be compound, made up of two or more words joined by a conjunction.

Ed and *she* are athletes.

The subject may be modified, or described, by words, phrases, or clauses.

That *ice* on the steps melted.

Practice: Underline the subject in each sentence.
1. Jacqueline and she are both photographers.
2. The empty house at the corner burned completely.
3. Their work was finished in only a few hours.
4. Chris Evert has won many tennis tournaments.

100

Verb

▷ GUIDE 5   The verb of a sentence is a word or phrase that expresses the action or state of being of the subject.

The sky glows.   *Isaac* can mail *the letter.*   Did *Toni Morrison* write *it?*

The verb may be compound, made up of two or more words joined by a conjunction.

She sang *and* played *the guitar.*

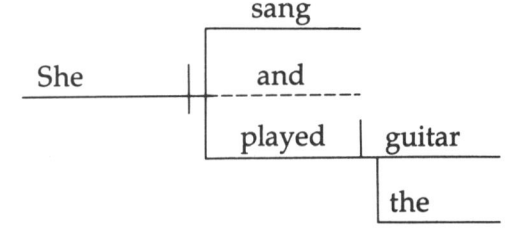

The verb may be modified, or described, by words, phrases, or clauses.

Her guitar was *not* damaged *in the fire.*

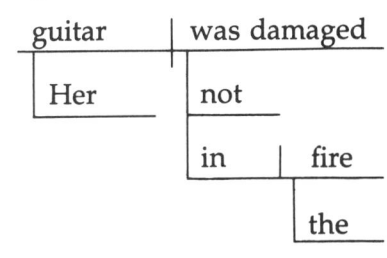

Practice: Underline the verb in each sentence.

1. It has been raining for hours.
2. Thunder crashed and banged.
3. Have they listened to the news?
4. A flood was reported in Ohio.

Answers to Practice Exercises, Pages 100 and 101

Guide 3
1. The clack of a typewriter came from upstairs.
2. You just must read this new book of science fiction.

Guide 4
1. Jacqueline, she
2. house
3. work
4. Chris Evert

Guide 5
1. has been raining
2. crashed, banged
3. Have, listened
4. was reported

Correct any mistakes.

101

Object

▷ GUIDE 6 **The direct object is the word that receives the action expressed by the verb.**

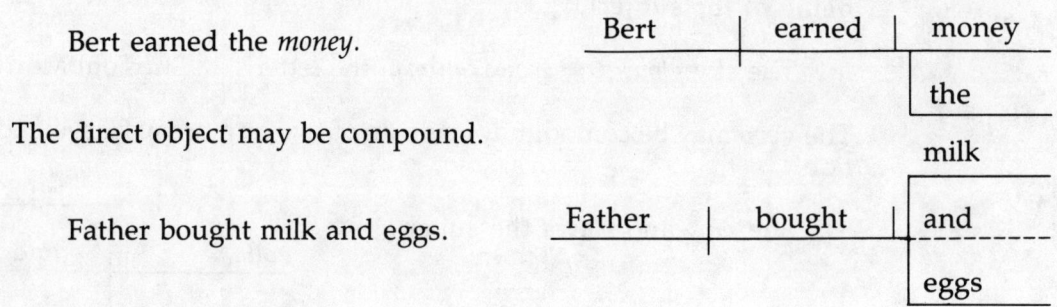

Bert earned the *money*.

The direct object may be compound.

Father bought milk and eggs.

Practice: Underline the direct objects in the sentences.
1. Shoko had read the newspaper ads.
2. He found a job last Wednesday.
3. Mr. Prochek hired him and Sonja.
4. He needs more experience.

▷ GUIDE 7 **The indirect object is the word that names to whom or for whom an action is done.**

The indirect object comes before the direct object in a sentence; it may be compound.

Ardell knitted *Meg* these gloves.

Practice: Underline the indirect objects in the sentences.
1. Yoshiko offered him some popcorn.
2. The foghorn gave them a warning.
3. He sold Jaime and Tom some new shirts.
4. We sent our friends the snapshots.

Subjective Complement

▷ GUIDE 8a **Subjective complements are predicate nominatives and predicate adjectives. The predicate nominative is a noun or pronoun that completes the verb and refers to the same person or thing as the subject.**

A noun used as a predicate nominative is commonly called a predicate noun. Predicate nominatives may be compound.

It was *they* who called.

He is a *sailor* and *diver*.

102

Practice: Underline the predicate nouns in the sentences.

1. Mrs. Rubin was his sister.
2. Are they friends or enemies?
3. These unusual flowers are orchids.
4. Georgia O'Keefe is a painter.

8b **The predicate adjective is a word that completes the verb and modifies, or describes, the subject.**

That must have been *exciting*.

Predicate adjectives may be compound.

Mark is tall and thin.

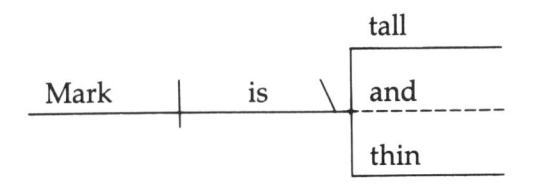

Practice: Underline the predicate adjectives in the sentences.

1. Those old buildings are unsafe.
2. Last night's movie was very dull.
3. Every speech had been very short.
4. One armchair is bright red.

Answers to Practice Exercises, Pages 102 and 103

Guide 6
1. ads
2. job
3. him, Sonja
4. experience

Guide 7
1. him
2. them
3. Jaime, Tom
4. friends

Guide 8a
1. sister
2. friends, enemies
3. orchids
4. painter

Guide 8b
1. unsafe
2. dull
3. short
4. red

Correct any mistakes.

103

SENTENCE STRUCTURE

The Simple Sentence

▷ GUIDE 9 **The simple sentence has one subject and one verb.**

Both the subject and verb may be compound, and they may be modified by other words.

Troy ran.
Troy, terrified, ran down the street.
Troy and Bill heard the explosion and ran.

Practice: Underline each subject once and each verb twice.

1. Tina and Azar have been here.
2. They laughed and joked all evening.
3. Our amusing visit was ended suddenly.
4. We enjoyed their company.

The Compound Sentence

▷ GUIDE 10 **The compound sentence is made up of two or more simple sentences that are usually connected by the conjunctions *or*, *and*, *so*, or *but*.**

Put a comma before the conjunction in a compound sentence.

You must hurry, *or* we will be late.

| You | must hurry || or || we | will be \ late |

I have tickets, *but* I can't go to the game.

Kim can go, *and* she will enjoy it.

Practice: Put a comma where it is needed in each sentence.

1. Greta called but she left no message.
2. Will you call or shall I?
3. The phone rang and she answered.
4. He and I left and we won't return.

The Complex Sentence

▷ GUIDE 11a **The complex sentence is made up of a main clause and one or more dependent clauses.**

When she spoke, I responded.

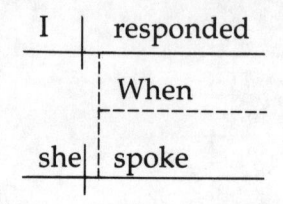

| I | responded |
| When |
| she | spoke |

(main clause: I responded)
(dependent clause: When she spoke)

When she spoke is an adverbial clause telling *when* the action took place in the main clause.

The answer that he gave was right.   (main clause: The answer was right)
(dependent clause: that he gave)

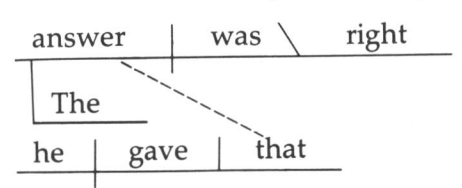

```
answer  |  was  \  right
   \The                \
    he | gave | that
```

That he gave is an adjectival clause modifying the subject of the main clause.

11b A dependent clause has a subject-verb relationship, but it is not a complete thought; it depends on the rest of the sentence for its meaning.

A dependent clause usually begins with one of the following introductory words: after, although, as, because, if, since, than, that, though, unless, until, what, when, where, which, while, who, whose. When a dependent clause appears at the beginning of a sentence, it is usually followed by a comma.

I found *what* I wanted.
While I was walking, I looked at the trees.
I haven't seen him *since* we discussed it.

Note: The introductory word of a dependent clause may take the place of the subject, and in some dependent clauses part of the subject-verb relationship is understood but does not appear.

They are the workers *who* built this bridge.
I am older *than* Felicia (is old).

Practice: Underline the dependent clause in each sentence.

1. If I ever get enough money, I am going to fly around the world.
2. Although you think I'm daydreaming, I'll see the world someday.
3. Since you're so sure of it, I wish you lots of luck.
4. Could you be a little envious because you didn't think of it first?
5. No, it's just something that I never had any ambition to do.

Answers to Practice Exercises, Pages 104 and 105

Guide 9
1. Tina and Azar have been here.
2. They laughed and joked all evening.
3. Our amusing visit was ended suddenly.
4. We enjoyed their company.

Guide 10
1. Greta called, but she left no message.
2. Will you call, or shall I?
3. The phone rang, and she answered.
4. He and I left, and we won't return.

Guides 11a, b
1. If I ever get enough money
2. Although you think I'm daydreaming
3. Since you're so sure of it
4. because you didn't think of it first
5. that I never had any ambition to do

Correct any mistakes.

PARTS OF SPEECH

Nouns

▷ GUIDE 12 **A noun is a word that names a person, place, thing, or idea.**

A common noun is the general name of a person, place, thing, or idea. A numeral, such as year, is also a common noun.

  man (person) town (place) engine (thing) truth (idea)

A proper noun is the name of a particular person, group, place, or thing.

  Luis Diaz (person) Mount Scott (place) Memorial Library (thing)

Practice: Underline the common and proper nouns in the sentences.

1. In the early days of our country there were many boats on the rivers.
2. The Mississippi was a very busy river then, as it is in our time.
3. Another busy and famous waterway was named for an explorer, Henry Hudson.
4. Planes, trains, and trucks now carry many products once hauled by ships.

▷ GUIDE 13 **A singular noun names one person, place, thing, or quality; a plural noun names more than one.**

  Singular: nail, kindness, cat Plural: nails, kindnesses, cats

There are many ways to form plural nouns. Some of the most common are listed below. Use a dictionary to find others.

(a) Add *s* to the singular from of a noun.
  chimney chimneys page pages jar jars wall walls

(b) Add *es* to nouns ending in *ch, sh, s, x,* or *z*.
  hitch hitches ax axes toss tosses wish wishes

(c) Replace the *y* with *i* and add *es* to nouns ending in *y* preceded by a consonant letter.
  caddy caddies sky skies candy candies ruby rubies

Practice: Write the plural form of each noun.

1. spy _____ 4. mass _____

2. lash _____ 5. use _____

3. alley _____ 6. attic _____

▷ **GUIDE 14** **The possessive form of a noun shows ownership or possession.**

To form the possessive of a singular noun, add an apostrophe and an *s*.

Jess's hat   the *team's* score   the *ship's* engine

To form the possessive of a plural noun ending in *s*, add an apostrophe only.

girls' houses   *cities'* governments

If the plural does not end in *s*, add an apostrophe and an *s*.

men's coats

Practice: Write the possessive form of each noun.

1. children _____   4. crowd _____

2. factories _____   5. boss _____

3. papers _____   6. women _____

Answers to Practice Exercises, Pages 106 and 107

Guide 12
1. days, country, boats, rivers
2. Mississippi, river, time
3. waterway, explorer, Henry Hudson
4. Planes, trains, trucks, products, ships

Guide 13
1. spies   4. masses
2. lashes   5. uses
3. alleys   6. attics

Guide 14
1. children's   4. crowd's
2. factories'   5. boss's
3. papers'   6. women's

Correct any mistakes.

Pronouns

▷ GUIDE   **15a**   **A pronoun is a word used in place of a noun.**

A personal pronoun takes the place of a definite person or thing. More than one pronoun or a pronoun and a noun may be used together.

    They went with me.   Evelyn and I were late.   We saw them.

The following are personal pronouns used to take the place of nouns:

Subject forms: I, you, he, she, it, we, they
Object forms: me, you, him, her, it, us, them
Possessive forms: my, mine, your, yours, his, her, hers, its, our, ours, their, theirs, whose*

*Remember that *its, their, theirs, whose, your,* and *yours* do not contain apostrophes. Do not confuse these pronouns with such words as *it's, there, they're, there's, who's,* and *you're.*

Practice: Underline the pronouns in the sentences.
1. Will you tell them why we have postponed our trip to the zoo?
2. I wanted to speak to him and her before my departure.

     15b   **For the subject of a sentence use one or more of the subject pronouns: I, you, he, she, it, we, they.**

The subject forms are also used after forms of the verb *be.*

    She is a good actress. It was *he* who played the part.

Note: When using one or more pronouns with the pronoun *I,* place the pronoun *I* last.

    He and I caught twenty fish.

Practice: Underline the subject pronouns in parentheses.
1. (We, Us) have a new television set.   3. (He, Him) and I liked the documentary.
2. It was (they, them) we invited.   4. (She, Her) and I are old friends.

     15c   **For the direct object or indirect object in a sentence, use one or more of the object pronouns: me, you, him, her, it, us, them.**

    Hamid invited *me* to lunch. Ruth gave *him* and *me* a lecture.

Note: When using one or more nouns or pronouns with the pronoun *me,* place the pronoun *me* last.

    Our boat gives Jacob and me much pleasure.

Practice: Underline the appropriate pronoun in parentheses.
1. This riddle gave (we, us) a laugh.
2. We saw (she, her) at the ski lodge.
3. I asked (they, them) about it.
4. We told him and (she, her) about it.

> **15d** **For the object of a preposition in a sentence use one or more of the object pronouns: me, you, him, her, it, us, them.**

Will Teresa go with Mario and *me*? We got a card for *them*.

Note: When using two or more pronouns after a preposition, read the sentence with one pronoun at a time in order to decide which forms to use.

The plants are for (*he* or *him*?) and (*I* or *me*?).
The plants are for *him* (not *he*.).
The plants are for *me* (not *I*).
The plants are for *him* and *me*.

Practice: Underline the appropriate pronoun in parentheses.
1. The dog barked at Bob and (I, me).
2. It was funny to her and (they, them).
3. With (he, him) were two senators.
4. Any book by (she, her) is a thriller.

Answers to Practice Exercises, Pages 108 and 109

Guide 15a
1. you, them, we, our
2. I, him, her, my

Guide 15b
1. We   3. He
2. they   4. She

Guide 15c
1. us   3. them
2. her   4. her

Guide 15d
1. me   3. him
2. them   4. her

Correct any mistakes.

109

15e **The pronoun and the word to which it refers (antecedent) must agree.**

>*Stella* can solve *her* own problems.
>Each of the women does *her* own work.
>The *people* shouted *their* choices.

Practice: Supply the pronoun that agrees with the antecedent.

1. Benito and Ted own _____ service garage.

2. Each of them has _____ favorite customers.

3. Ms. Adams won't let another mechanic repair _____ 1929 Pierce Arrow.

4. Many satisfied customers always take _____ cars to Benito and Ted.

▷ GUIDE 16 **A compound personal pronoun is a pronoun to which the word *self* or *selves* has been added.**

>If the pronoun refers to a singular noun, add the word *self*. If the pronoun refers to a plural noun, add the word *selves*.
>
>*Koji* put out the fire by *himself*.   The *owners* saved *themselves*.
>
>Note: Use *himself, themselves,* or *ourselves*, never *hisself, theirselves,* or *ourself*.

Practice: Supply the appropriate compound personal pronoun.

1. Now I want all of you to enjoy _____.

2. Morris was afraid to drive by _____ after dark.

3. Susan told me this _____.

▷ GUIDE 17 **An interrogative pronoun is a pronoun used in asking a question: what, who, whom, which, whose.**

>*Who* slammed the door?   *Which* one was it?   *Whose* pie is this?

Practice: Underline the interrogative pronouns.
1. Who will volunteer?
2. Whose money paid for it?
3. Which one did you choose?
4. Who said that I was wrong?

▷ GUIDE 18 **A demonstrative pronoun is a pronoun used to point out a person, place, or thing: this, that, these, those.**

>*This* is the skyscraper.   *These* belong to me.

Practice: Underline the demonstrative pronouns.
1. Who put that in my soup?
2. Those certainly look silly on a hat.
3. This is just too much!
4. Have you seen these?

▷ GUIDE *19* **An indefinite pronoun is a pronoun that refers to persons and things not definitely identified.**

Indefinite pronouns are such pronouns as the following: someone, anyone, one, each, all, everyone, some, none, either.

All of us hear it.   *Everyone* has books.

Practice: Underline the indefinite pronouns.

1. Someone is standing on my foot.
2. All of them denied it.
3. Is anyone listening to me?
4. Some of you should pay attention.

Answers to Practice Exercises, Pages 110 and 111

Guide 15e
1. their   3. her
2. his   4. their

Guide 16
1. yourselves   3. herself
2. himself

Guide 17
1. Who   3. Which
2. Whose   4. Who

Guide 18
1. that   3. This
2. Those   4. these

Guide 19
1. Someone   3. anyone
2. All   4. Some

Correct any mistakes.

111

▷ GUIDE 20 **A possessive pronoun is a pronoun that indicates ownership or a close relationship: my, mine, our, ours, your, yours, his, her, hers, its, their, theirs.**

>This diary is *mine*.   I thought it was *yours*.

Practice: Underline the possessive pronouns.

1. Will Caleb lend me his camera?
2. Mine has no film in it.
3. This one has lost its flash attachment.
4. Borrow one of theirs.

▷ GUIDE 21 **A relative pronoun is a pronoun used to introduce an adjective clause in a complex sentence: who, whom, which, that, whose.**

>The person *who* did this was an artist.
>The car *that* he bought was an old one.

Practice: Underline the relative pronouns.

1. Are you the person whose name was called?
2. Alice gave me a book, which I read immediately.
3. Bill wants a dog that will learn tricks.

Verbs

▷ GUIDE 22 **A verb shows action, being, or state of being.**

>A verb may be one or more words. The verb usually follows the subject in a sentence, but words of a verb may be separated by other words in a sentence.

>Ahmad *is* a player. (being)
>He *plays* for the Bruins. (action)
>He *seems* enthusiastic. (state of being)
>He *should have been made* captain. (four-word verb phrase)
>*Was* he *chosen* last year? (separated two-word verb phrase)

Practice: Underline the verb in each sentence.

1. Is Monica being sent as a representative?
2. Sally will not be going.
3. Craig represented us last time.
4. He was elected unanimously.

Kinds of Verbs

▷ GUIDE 23a **A verb may express a complete action (intransitive verb).**

>The dress *shrank*.   The boys *swim*.   The water pipes *froze*.

23b **A verb may need an object to express a complete action (transitive verb).**

>The farmer *raised corn*.   We *built* the *greenhouse*.
>They *gave us* the broom.   She *won* the *election*.

23c **A verb may need a subjective complement to express a complete action (linking verb).**

    He *seems unhappy*.   I *am hungry*.
    Mack *is* a *superintendent*. This cookie *tastes* too *sweet*.

Practice: After each of the following sentences, write *I* if the verb is intransitive, *T* if it is transitive, or *L* if it is linking.

1. This music sounds happy. _____

2. All of the girls skated. _____

3. Carl dropped the eggs. _____

Voice of Verbs

▷ GUIDE *24a* **A verb is in the active voice when the subject performs the action in a sentence.**

    A bee *stung* me. Patrick *swept* the walk. We *hailed* a taxi.

  24b **A verb is in the passive voice when the subject is acted upon.**

   When a verb is passive, the action is often performed by the object of the preposition.

    I *was stung* by a bee. The walk *was swept*.

Practice: Write the following sentence so that the verb is in the active voice.

1. The high pop fly to center field was hit by Mark.

Answers to Practice Exercises, Pages 112 and 113

Guide 20
1. his 3. its
2. Mine 4. theirs

Guide 21
1. whose 2. which 3. that

Guide 22
1. Is being sent 3. represented
2. will be going 4. was elected

Guides 23 a, b, c
1. L 2. I 3. T

Guides 24a, b
1. Mark hit the high pop fly to center field.

Correct any mistakes.

113

Agreement of Verbs

▷ GUIDE **25a A verb must agree with the subject in a sentence.**

Use singular subject-verb agreement with a singular subject; use plural subject-verb agreement with a plural subject or with a compound subject.

Singular	Plural
Her dog *is* a beagle.	Her dogs *are* beagles.
Bob *goes* to night school.	Bob and Ike *go* to night school.
She *has* no tractor.	They *have* tractors.
I *am* tired.	We *are* tired.
He *does* not *live* here.	They *do* not *live* here.
One of them *owns* a car.	All of us *own* cars.

Practice: Underline the verb that agrees with the subject.

1. They (want, wants) to meet you.
2. I (am, are) eager to know them, too.
3. (Do, Does) he remember Marty?
4. She (lives, live) next door to us.

25b Always use *are* or *were* (never *is* or *was*) with the pronoun *you*, whether it refers to one person or more than one.

You *are* a careful worker.   *Are* you three the typists they sent?

Practice: Underline the appropriate verb.

1. (Is, Are) all of you stenographers?
2. You (are, is) to take this chair.

25c Use *there is* or *there was* with a singular subject; use *there are* or *there were* with a plural or compound subject.

Is there anyone who doesn't like movies?
There are several plays that I want to see.
There were Joe and Cindy at the ticket window.

Practice: Underline the appropriate verb.

1. (Is, Are) there any seats here?
2. There (is, are) one in this row.

25d When the parts of a compound subject are connected by the conjunction *and*, subject-verb agreement is plural; when they are connected by the conjunction *or*, the verb agrees with the subject nearest the verb.

Vern, Bianca, and I *are* applicants for the job.
Two small trucks or one large truck *delivers* the mail.

Sometimes the compound subject follows the verb.

In the office *are* a typewriter and three adding machines.

Practice: Underline the appropriate verb.

1. Hassan and Phil (is, are) racing fans.
2. Cars, drivers, or a race (is, are) all they can talk about.

Principal Parts of Verbs

▷ GUIDE 26 **Each verb has a present participle and the following principal parts: present, past, past participle.**

The present is sometimes used with a helping verb. The present participle and past participle must be used with one or more helping verbs. The past is never used with a helping verb. The following are verbs that may be used as helping verbs:

am	are	is	been	may	shall	might	should
be	can	had	being	was	will	ought	would
do	did	has	must	have	were	could	

(The principal parts of some verbs are listed on the next page.)

Answers to Practice Exercises, Pages 114 and 115

Guide 25a
1. want
2. am
3. Does
4. lives

Guide 25b
1. Are   2. are

Guide 25c
1. Are   2. is

Guide 25d
1. are   2. is

Correct any mistakes.

The following are the principal parts of some verbs:

Present	Past	Past Participle	Present Participle
(may have a helping verb)	(never has a helping verb)	(must have helping verbs)	(must have helping verbs)
agree	agreed	agreed	agreeing
begin	began	begun	beginning
blow	blew	blown	blowing
break	broke	broken	breaking
carry	carried	carried	carrying
catch	caught	caught	catching
choose	chose	chosen	choosing
come	came	come	coming
count	counted	counted	counting
do	did	done	doing
draw	drew	drawn	drawing
drink	drank	drunk	drinking
drive	drove	driven	driving
eat	ate	eaten	eating
fill	filled	filled	filling
find	found	found	finding
fly	flew	flown	flying
forget	forgot	forgotten	forgetting
give	gave	given	giving
go	went	gone	going
guarantee	guaranteed	guaranteed	guaranteeing
hate	hated	hated	hating
hear	heard	heard	hearing
inflict	inflicted	inflicted	inflicting
know	knew	known	knowing
lay	laid	laid	laying
lie	lay	lain	lying
make	made	made	making
match	matched	matched	matching
pay	paid	paid	paying
plan	planned	planned	planning
promise	promised	promised	promising
save	saved	saved	saving
say	said	said	saying
see	saw	seen	seeing
set	set	set	setting
sign	signed	signed	signing
sit	sat	sat	sitting
speak	spoke	spoken	speaking
spy	spied	spied	spying
stop	stopped	stopped	stopping
take	took	taken	taking
throw	threw	thrown	throwing
tie	tied	tied	tying
travel	traveled	traveled	traveling
use	used	used	using
wear	wore	worn	wearing
write	wrote	written	writing

Verb Tenses

▷ GUIDE 27   The tense of a verb indicates the time of action or being.

Use verbs in present tenses to express action or being now. (Present perfect tense expresses action continuing until now.)

Present Tenses	I	he, she, it	we, you, they
Present	go	goes	go
Progressive	am going	is going	are going
Perfect	have gone	has gone	have gone

I *go* shopping after work.   She *is going* tonight.   *Have* they *gone*?

Use verbs in past tenses to express action or being in the past.

Past Tenses	I	he, she, it	we, you, they
Past	went	went	went
Progressive	was going	was going	were going
Perfect	had gone	had gone	had gone

I *went* there yesterday.   He *had* already *gone*.   He said that you *were going*.

Use verbs in future tenses to express action or being at a later time.

Future Tenses	I	he, she, it	we	you, they
Future	will go	will go	will go	will go
Progressive	will be going	will be going	will be going	will be going
Perfect	will have gone	will have gone	will have gone	will have gone

I *will have gone* by then.   It *will go* quickly.   *Will* we all *have gone*?

Practice: In each sentence tell whether the time expressed is present, past, or future.

1. Rey-Ling needs a new winter coat.   _____

2. Her money will all be spent before Saturday. _____

3. They went shopping last week.   _____

Answers to Practice Exercises, Page 117
1. present   2. future   3. past

Correct any mistakes.

Verbals

▷ GUIDE **28a** Verbals are verb forms that are used as adjectives, nouns, or adverbs. A participle is the present or past participle of a verb used as an adjective.

>The man *painting* is Mr. Noel.
>The *carved, painted* chair belongs to Margie.

Practice: Underline the participles in the sentences.

1. Mei-Li wore some warm, knitted gloves as he worked in the icy wind.
2. The freezing weather makes the repair work very difficult.
3. Many problems with telephones are caused by the sagging, iced wires.
4. Worn lines may break because of the additional weight of the ice.

28b A participle may be part of a participial phrase; the whole phrase is used as an adjective.

>The man *painting the house* is Mr. Noel. (modifies *man*)
>We saw a picture *painted in 1680*. (modifies *picture*)
>*Running swiftly*, the deer disappeared. (modifies *deer*)

Practice: Underline the participial phrase in each sentence.

1. The song played by the band is one of my favorites.
2. Did you notice the girl singing with the group?
3. Listening attentively, the people were very quiet.
4. When the music got lively, we heard many people clapping their hands.

28c A gerund is the *-ing* form of a verb used as a noun.

>*Swimming* builds arm and leg muscles. (gerund used as a subject)
>Nora teaches *swimming*. (gerund used as a direct object)

Practice: Underline the gerund in each sentence.

1. Reading is a favorite hobby at our house.
2. Of course, we all enjoy singing, too.
3. Have you ever tried skiing?
4. Skydiving is fun, also.

28d A gerund may be part of a gerund phrase; the whole phrase is used as a noun.

>*Swimming the English Channel* is a publicity stunt.
>Morris enjoys *swimming across the pond*.

Practice: Underline the gerund phrase in each sentence.
1. Painting the house kept us busy last summer.
2. I didn't mind slapping on paint.
3. Cleaning up the mess afterward was the part I dreaded.
4. Every evening I got the job of washing the paintbrushes.

28e An infinitive is the word *to* with a verb; it may be used as an adjective, an adverb, or a noun.

To act is his ambition. (infinitive used as a subject)
She had always wanted *to fly*. (infinitive used as a direct object)
Yesterday was a day *to remember*. (infinitive used as an adjective)
I was eager *to begin*. (infinitive used as an adverb)

Practice: Underline the infinitive in each sentence.
1. It was eight o'clock before Corkie decided to leave.
2. First she tried to skate with her friend.
3. Then she ambled inside to eat.
4. To hurry is simply not Corkie's way of doing things.

Answers to Practice Exercises, Pages 118 and 119

Guide 28a
1. knitted
2. freezing
3. sagging, iced
4. Worn

Guide 28b
1. played by the band
2. singing with the group
3. Listening attentively
4. clapping their hands

Guide 28c
1. Reading
2. singing
3. skiing
4. Skydiving

Guide 28d
1. Painting the house
2. slapping on paint
3. Cleaning up the mess afterward
4. washing the paintbrushes

Guide 28e
1. to leave   2. to skate   3. to eat   4. To hurry

Correct any mistakes.

28f An infinitive may be part of an infinitive phrase; the whole phrase is used as an adjective, an adverb, or a noun.

> She had always wanted *to fly through space.*
> *To act in the theater* was his ambition.
> Yesterday was a day *to remember forever.*
> I was eager *to begin my new job.*

Practice: Underline the infinitive phrase in each sentence.

1. To take criticism of our actions is difficult for most of us.
2. Most of us are eager to suggest improvements in other people.
3. However, we may not readily see the need to improve ourselves.
4. Would someone like to explain this difficulty?

Contractions

▷ GUIDE 29 **A contraction is a word formed by combining a verb and an adverb, a noun and a verb, or a pronoun and a verb.**

In a contraction one or more letters of the two words have been left out and an apostrophe put in their place.

> I *haven't* (have not) read the reviews.

The following are contractions; the words in parentheses are the words from which the contraction is formed.

isn't (is not)	we've (we have)	you'd (you would)
don't (do not)	you'll (you will)	who's (who is)
won't (will not)*	you'd (you had)	what's (what is)
it's (it is)	I'll (I shall)	he's (he is)
doesn't (does not)	we'd (we had)	there's (there is)
you're (you are)	he'll (he will)	they're (they are)
haven't (have not)	hasn't (has not)	they'll (they will)

*The contraction *won't* is formed differently from other contractions.

Practice: Write the contraction of each pair of words.

1. that is _____
2. are not _____
3. I am _____
4. we are _____
5. we had _____
6. she is _____

Troublesome Verbs

▷ GUIDE *30*   The verb *teach* means to give instruction.

The verb *learn* means to receive instruction or to find out how to do something.

Mrs. Huang can *teach* you to ski.   I will never *learn* how to ski.

Practice: Fill the blank with *teach* or *learn*.

1. Will you _____ me to swim?
2. You can't _____ to swim in a day.

▷ GUIDE *31*   **The verb *sit* means to be seated.**

The verb *set* means to place or put.

Don't *sit* on that tack!   Just *set* that box on the floor.

Practice: Underline the appropriate word in parentheses.

1. (Sit, Set) in this comfortable chair.
2. Miguel (sits, sets) here often.
3. I (sat, set) here all morning.
4. You can (sit, set) your purse here.

Answers to Practice Exercises, Pages 120 and 121

Guide 28f
1. To take criticism of our actions
2. to suggest improvements in other people
3. to improve ourselves
4. to explain this difficulty

Guide 29
1. that's
2. aren't
3. I'm
4. we're
5. we'd
6. she's

Guide 30
1. teach   2. learn

Guide 31
1. Sit
2. sits
3. sat
4. set

Correct any mistakes.

▷ GUIDE **32a** **The verb *lie* means to rest, recline, or remain in one place.**

The principal parts of *lie* are *lie*, *lay*, and *lain*. The present participle is *lying*.

The dog is *lying* in the shade.   He *lay* there all afternoon.

Practice: Underline the appropriate word in parentheses.

1. Were you (laying, lying) down?   2. The injured man (lay, lie) quietly.

32b **The verb *lay* means to place or put.**

The principal parts of *lay* are *lay*, *laid*, and *laid*. The present participle is *laying*.

Lay your coat there.   Marisol *laid* her sweater on the cat.

Practice: Underline the appropriate word in parentheses.

1. Don't (lie, lay) your glasses there.   2. Were the pages (lay, laid) flat?

Adjectives

▷ GUIDE **33a** **An adjective modifies, or describes, a noun or pronoun; it tells what kind, how many, or which one.**

Omar has a *dangerous* job. (what kind)
He works *eight* hours. (how many)
The *larger* furnace was repaired. (which one)

```
  Omar  |  has  |  job
                |  dangerous
                |  a
```

Practice: Underline the adjectives in the sentences.

1. Mrs. Clancy has funny, old-time pictures.
2. They have belonged to her for fifty years.

33b **The words *the*, *a*, and *an* are articles; they also modify nouns.**

The article *a* is used before a word beginning with a consonant sound, and the article *an* is used before a word beginning with a vowel sound.

the job   *a* supervisor   *an* employee

Note: See diagram in Guide 33a.

Practice: Underline the articles in the sentence.

1. The job required a physical examination, an employment test, and a conference.

33c A demonstrative adjective points out a particular noun; it tells which one.

Demonstrative adjectives are *this, that, these,* and *those.*

This part is new.   Have *those* men left?   *That* table should be moved.

Note: Remember that *them* is never a demonstrative adjective.

Practice: Underline the demonstrative adjectives.
1. I'll trade you this bicycle for that one.   2. Those people are noisier than these people.

33d Possessive forms of nouns and pronouns may be used as adjectives to modify nouns.

the *ship's* sails   *his* voyage   *their* orders

Practice: Underline the possessive nouns and pronouns used as adjectives.
1. Andy told about his invention.
2. He made it from a car's engine.
3. It was partly Jenny's idea, too.
4. Will they get a patent on their gadget?

Answers to Practice Exercises, Pages 122 and 123

Guide 32a
1. lying   2. lay

Guide 32b
1. lay   2. laid

Guide 33a
1. funny, old-time   2. fifty

Guide 33b
1. The, a, an, a

Guide 33c
1. this, that   2. Those, these

Guide 33d
1. his
2. car's
3. Jenny's
4. their

Correct any mistakes.

33e Present participle and past participle forms of verbs may be used as adjectives to modify nouns.

a *thrilling* mystery   a *trained* mechanic

Practice: Underline the participles used as adjectives.
1. The foaming water tore at the bank.
2. The flooded field was useless.

33f Proper adjectives are adjectives made from proper nouns.

a Greek myth   the British ship   the French scientist

Practice: Underline the proper adjectives.
1. The English language contains many Latin words as well as Anglo-Saxon words.

33g An adjective (not an adverb) should be used to modify the subject after such verbs as *look, feel, smell, sound, seem, taste,* and forms of *be*.

Even though the adjective follows the verb, it modifies the subject.

You look *nice* (not *nicely*).   I feel *bad* (not *badly*).

Practice: Underline the appropriate word in parentheses.
1. Those tomatoes smell (bad, badly).
2. Your drum sounds too (loud, loudly).

Adverbs

▷ GUIDE **34a An adverb modifies, or describes, a verb; it tells how, when, or where.**

Tamara runs *fast*. (how)
They live *there*. (where)
Yesterday we saw them. (when)

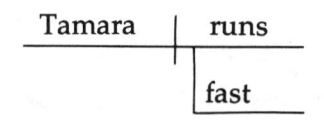

```
Tamara | runs
       |  fast
```

Practice: Underline the adverbs that modify verbs.
1. Loudly the door slammed.
2. She ran breathlessly up the walk.
3. People soon gathered at the corner.
4. Did I see you there?

34b An adverb may modify an adjective.

It was a *very* large ship. (modifes adjective *large*)
An *extremely* strong wind blew. (modifies adjective *strong*)

Practice: Underline the adverbs that modify adjectives.
1. That is quite useless information.
2. She is a most talented woman.
3. It is completely harmless talk.
4. She is a very busy mechanic.

34c An adverb may modify another adverb.

> We use this one *most* frequently. (modifies *frequently*)
> It is *very* widely used. (modifies *widely*)

Practice: Underline the adverbs that modify other adverbs.

1. Matt's cartoons are very well done.
2. You display that one quite proudly.
3. He works extremely fast.
4. A sketch is done almost instantly.

34d Many adverbs are formed by adding *ly* to an adjective.

> Do not confuse the adjectives *good* and *real* with the adverbs *well* and *very*.

Adjectives	Adverbs
She was *calm*.	She spoke *calmly*.
The sun is *bright*.	The sun shone *brightly*.
He did a *good* job.	He worked *well*.
It was a *real* surprise.	I was *really* surprised.
It gave me a *real* fright.	I was *very* frightened.

Practice: Underline the appropriate word in parentheses.

1. Dan did his work (happy, happily).
2. Jo Ann is a (calm, calmly) woman.
3. Marco is a (very, real) fine person.
4. Is this a (very, real) diamond?

Answers to Practice Exercises, Pages 124 and 125

Guide 33e
1. foaming   2. flooded

Guide 33f
1. English, Latin, Anglo-Saxon

Guide 33g
1. bad   2. loud

Guide 34a
1. Loudly   2. breathlessly   3. soon   4. there

Guide 34b
1. quite   2. most   3. completely   4. very

Guide 34c
1. very   2. quite   3. extremely   4. almost

Guide 34d
1. happily   2. calm   3. very   4. real

Correct any mistakes.

▷ GUIDE 35   **Do not use two negative adverbs (a double negative) in a sentence.**

Negatives are such words as *no, not, never,* and *hardly.*

> Roger *has* no faults.
> Roger *hasn't any* faults.
> Roger *hasn't a* fault.
>   (not: Roger *hasn't no* faults.)

Practice: Underline the appropriate word in parentheses.

1. She is hardly (ever, never) home.
2. She hasn't (no, any) free time.
3. It's not (a, no) surprise to me.
4. I can't see (any, no) sense in it.

Prepositions

▷ GUIDE 36a   **A preposition is a word that connects a noun or pronoun to the rest of the sentence.**

The noun or pronoun that follows the preposition is the object of the preposition.

> He fell *through* the step. (preposition *through* connects *step* to the rest of the sentence)
> I fell *beside* him. (preposition *beside* connects pronoun *him* to the rest of the sentence)

The following are common prepositions:

about	among	beside	from	of	over	up
across	around	between	in	off	under	with
after	at	by	inside	on	to	within
above	behind	for	near	outside	through	without

Practice: Underline the prepositions in the sentence.

1. In and around the grape arbor under the window many moths darted.

36b   **A prepositional phrase includes the preposition, the object of the preposition, and any words that modify the object of the preposition.**

> The rabbit hid *under the tall, dry grass.* (object *grass*)
> Lucia fished *with John and me.* (compound object *John, me*)
> My parents were married *in 1961.* (object *1961*)

Practice: Underline the prepositional phrases.

1. In the gloom of the evening the lonely man walked along the Thames.
2. Under his arm he carried a goose that had lately been deprived of its feathers.
3. In 1814 a famous battle was fought in New Orleans.

36c A prepositional phrase that explains or modifies a noun or pronoun is used as an adjective; it tells which one or what kind.

Cards *in the blue box* are his.

```
Cards  |  are  \  his
   in  |  box
           blue
           the
```

Practice: Underline the prepositional phrase used as an adjective; put parentheses around the noun it modifies.

1. Have you read this article about charge accounts?
2. You sometimes pay a high rate of interest.
3. This interest charge raises the price of every purchase.
4. The cost for charging purchases may be more than you expected.

Answers to Practice Exercises, Pages 126 and 127

Guide 35
1. ever   3. a
2. any   4. any

Guide 36a
1. In, around, under

Guide 36b
1. In the gloom, of the evening, along the Thames
2. Under his arm, of its feathers
3. In 1814, in New Orleans

Guide 36c
1. (article) about charge accounts   3. (price) of every purchase
2. (rate) of interest   4. (cost) for charging purchases

Correct any mistakes.

127

36d A prepositional phrase that explains or modifies a verb is used as an adverb; it tells how, when, or where.

The leaves scattered *in the wind*.

```
leaves  |  scattered
   \The      \in  \wind
                    \the
```

Practice: Underline the prepositional phrase used as an adverb; put parentheses around the verb it modifies.

1. The long, crimson racer swerved crazily from the track.
2. Through the white wooden railing it crashed.
3. Excited track officials ran to the smoking racer.
4. The lucky driver walked from the scene.

36e Some prepositions have particular meanings.

> between—usually refers to two persons or things (*in between* is incorrect)
> among—usually refers to more than two persons or things
> off—refers to physical separation (*off of* is incorrect)
> from—refers to beginning or source
> of—refers to ownership or possession
> in—refers to the state of being inside something
> into—refers to movement from the outside to the inside

Practice: Underline the appropriate preposition in parentheses.

1. We went (in, into) the shop.
2. I bought a hat (off, from) the woman.
3. (Between, Among) four we liked it best.
4. He carried the hat (in, into) a box.

Conjunctions

▷ GUIDE **37a** A coordinating conjunction connects words or groups of words in a sentence. Some conjunctions are *and, or, but,* and *so.* Sometimes conjunctions are used in pairs (*either/or; neither/nor*).

Nathan *and* Brian are brothers. *Neither* Alma *nor* Cathy was at home.

Subordinating conjunctions show such relationships as condition, time, cause, and effect. Some of these conjunctions are *when, until, where, because, after, while, although,* and *if.* They are used to introduce adverb clauses.

I bought the sweater. It was on sale.
I bought the sweater *because* it was on sale.

Practice: Underline the conjunctions in the following sentences.

1. Tom won't quit until he succeeds.
2. Robert sang and danced all night.
3. Either Karen or Bill will call you.
4. Sue jumped up when the bell rang.

37b Use a conjunction to combine short sentences.

Put a comma before the conjunction that joins a compound sentence.

Ted wanted to go. Felicia wanted to stay home.
Ted wanted to go, *but* Felicia wanted to stay home.

If a subordinating conjunction appears at the beginning of a sentence, the clause in which it occurs is set apart by a comma.

When the bell rang, Sue jumped up.

Practice: Combine each pair of short sentences to make one sentence. Use the conjunction in parentheses.

1. Peggy had better get to work on time. She will be fired. (or) _____

2. John was tired. He went dancing. (although) _____

37c Use conjunctions to connect compound elements.

Mateo is cheerful. He is witty. He is kind.
Mateo is cheerful, witty, *and* kind.

Practice: Combine the sentences into one sentence containing a compound element.

1. Glen drives the tractor. So does Jan. Don drives it, too.

Answers to Practice Exercises, Pages 128 and 129

Guide 36d
1. (swerved) from the track
2. Through the white wooden railing (crashed)
3. (ran) to the smoking racer
4. (walked) from the scene

Guide 36e
1. into   2. from   3. Among   4. in

Guide 37a
1. until   2. and   3. Either, or   4. when

Guide 37b
1. Peggy had better get to work on time, or she will be fired.
2. Although John was tired, he went dancing.

Guide 37c
1. Glen, Jan, and Don drive the tractor.
   (or: Glen and Jan and Don drive the tractor.)

Correct any mistakes.

Interjections

▷ GUIDE 38 **An interjection is a word that expresses strong or sudden emotion.**

Common interjections are *oh, ah, hi, hello, ouch, well, good,* and *indeed.*

Indeed! Who told you?
Well! How did you ever guess?

Practice: Underline the interjections.

1. Hello! How are you?
2. Good! It serves you right!

CAPITALIZATION

▷ GUIDE 39a **Use a capital letter to begin the first word of a sentence.**

Have you heard from your uncle in California?

39b **Use a capital letter to begin a proper noun. A proper noun is the name of a particular person, group, place, or thing.**

Ethel Waters	Baytown Medical School	*Discovery* (a ship)
King Albert I	American College of Surgeons	Civil War
Puerto Rico	Battle of Freeman's Farm	Hoover Dam
Hudson River	United States Congress	Smoky Mountains
East (a region)	General Hospital	Republicans
Williams' Market	Roosevelt Library	Chicago, Illinois

39c **Use a capital letter to begin a proper adjective.**

Spanish   African   Indian   French   American   Shakespearean

39d **Use a capital letter to begin the name of a day of the week.**

Monday   Tuesday   Wednesday   Thursday

39e **Use a capital letter to begin the name of a month. Do not capitalize a season.**

January   February   September   November   summer

39f **Use a capital letter to begin the name of a holiday or a special day.**

Mardi Gras   Labor Day   New Year's Day   Thanksgiving

39g **Capitalize the word *I*.**

I didn't think before I spoke.

Practice: Use appropriate capitalization.

1. gloria dean scott _____
2. united states of america _____
3. italian _____
4. museum of modern art _____
5. new york mets _____
6. fourth of july _____
7. october _____
8. did i see you on tuesday? _____

Answers to Practice Exercises, Pages 130 and 131

Guide 38
1. Hello!   2. Good!

Guides 39a–g
1. Gloria Dean Scott
2. United States of America
3. Italian
4. Museum of Modern Art
5. New York Mets
6. Fourth of July
7. October
8. Did I see you on Tuesday?

Correct any mistakes.

131

CAPITALIZATION AND PUNCTUATION

▷ **GUIDE 40** Capitalize an initial used in place of a name; put a period after the initial.

      A. T. Morton   Ann T. Morales   J. Cuthbert Ord

Practice: Write the following names appropriately.

1. g olen ross _____   2. v r welch _____

▷ **GUIDE 41** Use a capital letter to begin a title of respect. Put a period after an abbreviated title of respect.

A title of respect is a courtesy title used before a name.

    Mr. (Mister)   Mrs. (Mistress)   Dr. (Doctor)   Miss
    Ms. (written as an abbreviation, a title often used for a woman)

Practice: Write the following names appropriately.

1. miss melanie chambers _____   2. dr q z poe _____

▷ **GUIDE 42** Use a capital letter to begin an abbreviation for the name of a day or month. Put a period after the abbreviation.

Do not abbreviate May, June, or July.

    Wed. (Wednesday)   Oct. (October)

Practice: Write the following abbreviations appropriately.

1. thurs _____ 2. sept _____ 3. fri _____ 4. jan _____

▷ **GUIDE 43** Capitalize and punctuate addresses as shown below.

    Mr. C. M. Dunbar
    5701 Gladstone Drive
    Albuquerque, New Mexico 87105

Practice: Write the following address appropriately.

1. mrs hans lupke _____

   387 prospect place _____

   mason city iowa 50401 _____

▷ GUIDE **44** Use a capital letter to begin each abbreviation used in an address. Notice that most abbreviations made with two capital letters are not followed by a period.

        Co. (Company)   SW (Southwest)   Ave. (Avenue)   IL (Illinois)

Practice: Write the following address appropriately.

1. dr sara roberts

   medical bldg

   100 n commerce ave

   houston tx 77001

Answers to Practice Exercises, Pages 132 and 133

Guide 40
1. G. Olen Ross   2. V. R. Welch

Guide 41
1. Miss Melanie Chambers   2. Dr. Q. Z. Poe

Guide 42
1. Thurs.   2. Sept.   3. Fri.   4. Jan.

Guide 43
1. Mrs. Hans Lupke
   387 Prospect Place
   Mason City, Iowa 50401

Guide 44
1. Dr. Sara Roberts
   Medical Bldg.
   100 N. Commerce Ave.
   Houston, TX 77001

Correct any mistakes.

▷ GUIDE 45   When all or part of an address is given in a sentence, place commas as follows: after the name of the person or company, after the street address or box number, after the city, after the state or ZIP code, or after the country. If the address comes at the end of a sentence, use the correct end punctuation instead of a comma.

>   He moved to Washington, D.C., last month.
>   Alejandro Ruiz lived in Tucson, Arizona, most of his life.
>   How old a city is St. Augustine, Florida?
>   The ship left London, England, on Tuesday.
>   Write to Hall-Ark Company, Box 731, Dayton, Ohio 45401, today.

Practice: Punctuate the sentences.

1. Did Tony move to San Angelo Texas
2. Send the invoice to Samson Truck Company Box 12 Hartford Connecticut 06101
3. The weather in Houston Texas is often humid

▷ GUIDE 46   Use a capital letter to begin the first word and every important word in a title.

>   The Sound of Music   Life on the Mississippi

Place quotation marks around the following kinds of titles when they are part of a sentence: a short story, a short poem, a radio show, a televison show, a song.

>   He often sang the song "Reuben James."
>   Shelly wanted to hear "The Three Bears".

Underline the following kinds of titles when they are part of a sentence: a book, a long poem, a movie, a play, a painting, a magazine, a newspaper, a ship, an airplane.

>   Have you read today's <u>Washington Post</u>? Jessica is reading <u>True Grit</u>.

Practice: Punctuate the following titles.

1. Did Bret Harte write the story called The Outcasts of Poker Flat?
2. Saturday we saw Duck Soup, starring the Marx Brothers.

▷ GUIDE 47   Use a capital letter to begin the first word of a direct quotation. Put quotation marks around a direct quotation.

A direct quotation is the exact words of a speaker. When the speaker's name comes before a direct quotation, put a comma before the quotation. When the speaker's name comes after a direct quotation, put a comma, question mark, or exclamation point after the quotation. Put the punctuation mark at the end of a direct quotation inside the quotation marks.

>   Kay asked, "How far is it from Boston to New Haven?"
>   "I've never been east of Peoria," Will said.

Practice: Punctuate the sentence.

1. Troy said Somebody ate the piece of pie I was saving

OTHER USES OF THE COMMA

▷ GUIDE 48   In writing a date, put a comma between the day of the month and the year. If no day is given, put a comma between the month and the year. Put a comma between the name of the day of the week and the month.

January 1, 1978   January, 1978   Monday, January 1, 1978

In a sentence put a comma after the year unless the year comes at the end of the sentence. Put a comma after the day of the week and after the day of the month unless the day of the month comes at the end of the sentence.

On October 12, 1492, Columbus landed in the West Indies.
Margaret E. Kuhn founded the Gray Panthers in June, 1970.
On Saturday, December 6, they were in Washington.

Practice: Punctuate the dates in the sentences.

1. The date September 27 1943 was typed on both copies.
2. On Wednesday June 14 1988 this permit will expire.
3. Did Mr. James begin work on Monday March 27

Answers to Practice Exercises, Pages 134 and 135

Guide 45
1. Did Tony move to San Angelo, Texas?
2. Send the invoice to Samson Truck Company, Box 12, Hartford, Connecticut 06101.
3. The weather in Houston, Texas, is often humid.

Guide 46
1. Did Bret Harte write the story called "The Outcasts of Poker Flat"?
2. Saturday we saw <u>Duck Soup</u>, starring the Marx Brothers.

Guide 47
1. Troy said, "Somebody ate the piece of pie I was saving."

Guide 48
1. The date September 27, 1943, was typed on both copies.
2. On Wednesday, June 14, 1988, this permit will expire.
3. Did Mr. James begin work on Monday, March 27?

Correct any mistakes.

▷ GUIDE 49   In a sentence set off the name of the person addressed (direct address) with a comma or commas.

> Dan, have you worked here before?
> I worked here last summer, Mr. Clark.
> If I can help you, Dan, let me know.

Practice: Insert commas where they are needed.

1. Amelia please remember to sign your letters.
2. Thank you for reminding me Miss Hacker.
3. When these letters are typed Roger you may file the copies.

▷ GUIDE 50   Put a comma after the word *yes* or *no* at the beginning of a sentence.

> Yes, I distinctly heard him say it.
> No, she did not reply to my questions.

Practice: Insert commas where they are needed.

1. No you should not accept this defective machine.
2. Yes Simon I would return it to the manufacturer.

▷ GUIDE 51   Set off with commas such interrupting words as *however, of course,* and *too.*

> You know, *of course,* that she arrived yesterday.
> *However,* we were not expecting her.
> She will stay there a month, *too.*
> We were surprised, *too,* when she arrived.

Practice: Insert commas where they are needed.

1. Morgan of course likes to act like a very important man.
2. He has a way too of making people believe his stories.
3. You must examine very carefully everything he tells you however.

▷ GUIDE 52   Set off with commas words or phrases in a series.

> The tall, quiet man entered the room.
> Cal, Mickey, Wanda, and I spoke to him.
> He spoke to us, sat down, and started reading.

Practice: Insert commas where they are needed.

1. Karen Hal and I all work in the bookkeeping department.
2. We answer the phones type letters and greet customers.
3. Sandy is the quiet attractive woman at the first desk.

▷ GUIDE 53   **An appositive is often set off with a comma or commas.**

An appositive is an element that follows a noun and explains, identifies, or describes it. The appositive may be a single word or a group of words.

The announcer, *Jeff Wilson,* faced the TV cameras.
Outside the studio paced the eager contestants, *Hamid and Silvia.*
The grand prize, *a trip and a new automobile,* awaited today's winner.

Practice: Underline the appositive in each sentence.
1. The foreword, or introduction, is an important part of this book.
2. The welding instructor, Mr. Monroe, asked that we all read it.
3. He was a welder at Interair, the huge factory at Springfield.

Answers to Practice Exercises, Pages 136 and 137

Guide 49
1. Amelia, please remember to sign your letters.
2. Thank you for reminding me, Miss Hacker.
3. When these letters are typed, Roger, you may file the copies.

Guide 50
1. No, you should not accept this defective machine.
2. Yes, Simon, I would return it to the manufacturer.

Guide 51
1. Morgan, of course, likes to act like a very important man.
2. He has a way, too, of making people believe his stories.
3. You must examine very carefully everything he tells you, however.

Guide 52
1. Karen, Hal, and I all work in the bookkeeping department.
2. We answer the phones, type letters, and greet customers.
3. Sandy is the quiet, attractive woman at the first desk.

Guide 53
1. or introduction
2. Mr. Monroe
3. the huge factory at Springfield

Correct any mistakes.

137

THE PARAGRAPH

▷ GUIDE **54a** A paragraph is a group of sentences about one topic, or subject. A paragraph should include a sentence that tells the topic of the paragraph. This sentence is called the topic sentence.

My uncle Gus is the family clown. (topic sentence for a paragraph about a person)

Practice: Read the paragraph and answer the questions below it.

The first day on my new job, I was determined to work very hard. I arrived thirty minutes early because I wanted to make a good impression. I was given a chair and told to wait for the personnel manager. After my talk with him, I was sent to the company clinic for an examination. I waited while others were being examined. As soon as the doctor said I was healthy, I was sent in to see the shop supervisor. She was at her morning coffee break, so I waited for her. When she got back, she asked me about my work experience. Then she left, and I waited. Before long, every person in the shop left. I decided it must be lunchtime, but I stayed where I was. About one o'clock the shop supervisor came in and said she hoped I enjoyed my lunch. She took me on a tour of the shop and introduced me to the workers. While we were talking, the telephone in the shop office rang. The personnel office was calling to tell me I must fill out some more forms. I went back to the personnel office and waited until my name was called. As I signed the last form, I noticed the typists clearing their desks. It was quitting time.

1. What is the topic sentence of the paragraph? _____

2. What does the paragraph tell about the topic? _____

54b In writing a paragraph, follow the suggestions below.

If the paragraph has a title, capitalize the first word and every important word in the title. Indent the first sentence. Introduce the topic of the paragraph in an interesting topic sentence. Be sure that all sentences in the paragraph have some connection with the topic. Present ideas in the paragraph in some logical order. In the last sentence you may want to make a summary statement about the topic. Be sure to write complete sentences. Use capital letters and punctuation marks appropriately. Follow the rules of good grammar.

The following suggestions will help you write more interesting paragraphs.

Select a topic you know something about or about which you can find information. Try to begin sentences in different ways. Add interesting details to your sentences to give the reader a clear picture of the topic. Avoid using overworked words, such as "fine," "nice," and "good."

Practice: Underline the sentences that do not have a close connection with the topic sentence.

> The scene outside my window today is so attractive that I am neglecting my work. I have more work than I can do, anyhow. I squint in the glare of sunlight on fresh snow. A few strands of dry grass protrude through the snowy covering. They make skinny shadows in the winter sun. Dull-brown sparrows search unsuccessfully for bits of food on the white ground. People should put out food for the birds in winter. Before I finally turn back to my work, I cast one last, admiring glance at the icicles hanging from the roof.

Answers to Practice Exercises, Pages 138 and 139

Guide 54a
1. The first day on my new job, I was determined to work very hard.
2. The paragraph describes what happened the first day on a new job.

Guide 54b
I have more work than I can do, anyhow.
People should put out food for the birds in winter.

Correct any mistakes.

BUSINESS LETTERS

▷ GUIDE **55a** **A business, or formal, letter has six parts: heading, inside address, greeting, body, complimentary close, signature.**

The parts are arranged, capitalized, and punctuated as they appear in the following example.

Heading:	1421 Central Avenue Peoria, Illinois 61601 January 23, 1985
Inside address:	Ms. Jan Cato Cato Flight Service Box 369 Miami, Florida 33101
Optional greeting: Body:	Dear Ms. Cato: Please send me a copy of the chart "Jobs in Aviation," which was listed in <u>Aero</u> Magazine.
Complimentary close:	Yours truly,
Signature:	Jerome Hahn

Practice: List in order the six parts of a business letter.

1. _____ 4. _____

2. _____ 5. _____

3. _____ 6. _____

55b **In a business letter use a formal greeting and complimentary close and the full name of the person signing the letter.**

Capitalize and punctuate these parts of a business letter according to the following examples.

(a) Formal greeting: Dear Mr. Blank:
    (optional) Service Manager: (to a position)
    Customer Service: (to a department)

(b) Formal complimentary close: Sincerely yours,
    Very truly yours,
    Yours truly,

(c) Formal signature: Daniel Martin (full name)

Practice: Add an appropriate greeting and complimentary close to the letter.

1422 West Ninth Street
Laramie, Wyoming 82070
June 17, 1985

Mr. Harry Weston
Regal Cosmetics Company
642 West Simms Place
Grand Rapids, Michigan 49501

_____

Your ad in the June issue of <u>New Life</u> listed a fitted makeup case. Please let me know the price of the case and the charges for shipping.

_____

Alberta Louise Guerrero

Answers to Practice Exercises, Pages 140 and 141

Guide 55a
1. Heading
2. Inside address
3. Optional greeting
4. Body
5. Complimentary close
6. Signature

Guide 55b
Dear Mr. Weston:
Sincerely yours, (or: Very truly yours, or: Yours truly,)

Correct any mistakes.

141

ENVELOPES

▷ GUIDE 56 Follow the rules below in addressing an envelope.
(a) Put the return address (the address of the sender) in the upper left-hand corner of the envelope. Include the correct ZIP code.
(b) Near the center of the envelope put the name and address of the person or company to whom the letter is to be sent. Include the correct ZIP code.
(c) Punctuate and capitalize envelope addresses as shown in the following examples.

Peter J. Alonso
Box 136
Laramie, Wyoming 82070

　　　　　　　　　　　　　Mr. Terence Holloway
　　　　　　　　　　　　　642 Harndale Drive
　　　　　　　　　　　　　Gainesville, Texas 76240

Mrs. Mohammed Faisal
2815 Harmon Way
Dover, Delaware 19901

　　　　　　　　　　　　　Miss Evelyn Murphey
　　　　　　　　　　　　　716 McKinley Street
　　　　　　　　　　　　　Kingston, Rhode Island 02881

Practice: Address the envelope to Mr. Joseph Santez, 5396 Huntingdon Drive, Albany, New York 12201. Use the following return address: Gerhardt Meyer, 417 North Aluma, Buffalo, New York 14205.

Answers to Practice Exercise, Page 143

Guide 56

Gerhardt Meyer
417 North Aluma
Buffalo, New York 14205

                                      Mr. Joseph Santez
                                      5396 Huntingdon Drive
                                      Albany, New York 12201

Correct any mistakes.

THE DICTIONARY

▷ GUIDE **57a** Use a dictionary to obtain the following information about a word: spelling, pronunciation, syllable division, meaning.

Words in a dictionary are arranged in alphabetical order.

The pronunciation of a word is shown in a respelling after the entry word.

Stressed syllables are indicated by various kinds of accent marks.

Syllables are usually indicated by separations or marks in the entry word.

con·ven′tion

Practice: List four kinds of information a dictionary gives about a word.

1. _____   3. _____

2. _____   4. _____

57b Words in the dictionary are arranged in alphabetical order: a, b, c, d, e, f, g, h, i, j, k, l, m, n, o, p, q, r, s, t, u, v, w, x, y, z.

Words that begin with the same first letter are arranged in alphabetical order according to the second, third, and following letters.

antelope	ginger	mason	tiger
ashes	glass	milk	tulip
bell	hawk	nest	umbrella
cotton	hobby	opal	violin
dollar	ice	owl	wind
ear	icy	parrot	winter
eye	janitor	quail	xylophone
father	kangaroo	radio	yearly
fear	lawn	sailing	yearn
feather	leopard	sailor	zebra

Practice: Write the words in each group in alphabetical order.

1. valuable busy   occur   _____ _____ _____

2. does   believe forty   _____ _____ _____

3. know   author   afraid   _____ _____ _____

4. their   there   they   _____ _____ _____

5. hoping   hopping hope   _____ _____ _____

6. discuss   differ   desk   _____ _____ _____

57c When dividing a word at the end of a line of writing, divide it between syllables; never divide a word of one syllable.

Put a hyphen at the end of a syllable. Write the rest of the word on the next line.

    black (one syllable: do not divide)
    pa-per (two syllables)   in-no-cent (three syllables)

Practice: Underline the words that should not be divided.

1. straight
2. under
3. those
4. thrift
5. green
6. meadow
7. nineteen
8. bought
9. doorway
10. permanent
11. offer
12. through

57d A dictionary entry may include a synonym and/or antonym.

    tall [tôl] *adj.* Of more than average height. **Ant** see *short.* **Syn** see *high.*

▷ GUIDE 58 When filling out a form or taking a test, consider these guidelines: First, read all directions. Ask questions if the directions are not clear. Follow the directions carefully. If a question does not apply to you, write NA in the blank, for *not applicable.* If you do not know the answer to a question, make a dash in the blank. Neatly erase or mark out an incorrect answer. Then, write in the correct answer. Carry a list of credit and personal references, including account numbers, names, addresses, and telephone numbers.

WORDSEARCH

▷ GUIDE 59 Building word power helps you become a better listener and a better speaker.

WORDSEARCH will help you build word power. In each WORDSEARCH activity, you will find a group of four words in row 1. Use a dictionary to find the meanings of any of the words that you do not know. Then look at the three words in row 2. Select the word that is most closely related to the words in row 1. Write this word on the line. Be ready to take part in a discussion of the WORDSEARCH word.

Answers to Practice Exercises, Pages 144 and 145

Guide 57a
1. spelling   2. pronunciation   3. syllable division   4. meaning

Guide 57b
1. busy   occur   valuable   4. their   there   they
2. believe   does   forty   5. hope   hoping   hopping
3. afraid   author   know   6. desk   differ   discuss

Guide 57c
1. straight   3. those   4. thrift   5. green   8. bought   12. through

Correct any mistakes.

ANSWERS TO EXERCISES

Unit I
Lesson 1
Part I:
1. X
2. (.)
3. (.)
4. (.)
5. (?)
6. X
7. (.)
8. X
9. (?)
10. X
11. (?)
12. (.)

Part II: Answers will vary.
WORDSEARCH: medicine

Lesson 2
Part I:
1. (?) interrog.
2. (.) declar.
3. (!) exclam.
4. (.) imper.
5. (?) interrog.
6. (.) declar.
7. (?) interrog.
8. (!) exclam.
9. (?) interrog.
10. (.) declar.
11. (?) interrog.

Part II: Answers will vary.

Lesson 3
1. Camagüeyanos; won; championship*
2. men, women, children; line; streets
3. music, shouts; fill; air
4. jeeps; carry; heroes
5. voices; shout; cheers, slogans
6. everyone; welcomes; team
7. fans; are shouting; names
8. players; have beaten; teams
9. anyone; will forget; victory, celebration
10. players; will take; field

*For purposes of scoring, each sentence element will count as one point regardless of the number of words in the element.

Lesson 4
Part I: Predicate nouns will vary. Each sentence should be punctuated with a period.
1. animal.
2. meat. (or leaves.)
3. claws. (or teeth.)
4. country.
5. bear.
6. sight.
7. Alaska. (or Montana.)
8. beast.
9. food.

Part II:
10. She is industrious.
11. He was very artistic.
12. This movie is terrible.
13. That hiker was frightened.
14. My coat is green.
15. You are clever.
16. That ring is valuable.
17. Your apartment is large.
18. The day was extremely hot.

Lesson 5
Part I:
1. favorites; games; PN
2. moves; helpful; PA
3. games; new; PA
4. Montague Redgrave; wizard; PN
5. 1871; date; PN
6. game; mechanical; PA
7. game; favorite; PN
8. W. M. McManus; designer; PN
9. machines; popular; PA
10. inventor; maker; PN
11. versions; numerous; PA
12. Chicago; center; PN
13. figures; pretty; PA
14. games; source; PN
15. machines; valuable; PA

Part II: Answers will vary.

Lesson 6
1. The scared young man stepped into the elevator.
2. He thought he got stares from every person there.
3. He just had to have this job!
4. He had practiced what he would say.
5. He entered timidly through the heavy glass door.
6. The sounds of people at work burst all around him.
7. He must enter that office on the left.
8. The personnel manager sat behind the big desk.
9. He answered questions in a shaky voice.
10. She was so impressed that she hired the young man.

Lesson 7
Part I: (in order of appearance)
Are, seen, does, doesn't, aren't, is, was, has, is, think, call, has

Part II: Answers will vary.
WORDSEARCH: map

Lesson 8
The underlined words should be capitalized.
    Daniel Hale Williams was born in Hollidaysburg, Pennsylvania, in 1856. Left an orphan at twelve, he

Lessons 8 to 11

supported himself while he went to school. Then, with the help of friends in Chicago, Illinois, he entered Northwestern Medical School. Daniel Williams became a doctor in June, 1883.

Several years later he organized Provident Hospital in Chicago. One summer night a man with a wound in his heart was brought to the hospital. With the help of others, Dr. Williams closed the wound and saved the man's life. The skillful black surgeon had performed the first successful heart surgery. The year was 1893!

Freedman's Hospital in Washington, D.C., was operated by the United States government. Dr. Williams reorganized the hospital and made it one of the best of that time.

Lesson 9
Part I:
1. Tombstone, Arizona, was one of the wildest towns in the Old West.
2. Clara, who was Ed Schieffelin?
3. Wasn't he a slow, careful, persistent prospector?
4. Yes, Schieffelin had searched in Oregon, California, and Nevada with little success.
5. Then he began searching the hills near the San Pedro River in southern Arizona.
6. What a hot, dry, empty area that was!
7. How long Schieffelin searched without having any luck!
8. Rattlesnakes, Gila monsters, and bandits lurked in the rocky canyons.
9. Did Schieffelin say to a soldier that he would find something useful out there?
10. Yes, but what was the soldier's reply, Clara?
11. The soldier told Schieffelin that he would find one useful thing, his own tombstone.
12. Schieffelin, however, found a rich, wide, and promising vein of silver.
13. Was the name of the claim, The Tombstone, an answer to the soldier's cruel reply?
14. Soon the town of Tombstone, Arizona, was born.
15. Toughnut Street, Allen Street, Fremont Street, and Safford Street were laid out.
16. What happened on Wednesday, October 26, 1881, at the O.K. Corral?
17. Didn't Wyatt Earp, his brothers, and Doc Holliday duel Ike Clanton's cowhands?
18. "The town too tough to die" is still alive and kicking today, Clara.

Part II: Answers will vary.
COMPOSITION: Answers will vary.

Lesson 10
Part I:
1. (.) bison
2. X
3. X
4. (.) bison
5. (.) Settlers
6. X

Part II:
7. on april 1, 1981, we left for yellowstone national park.
8. did cara go with you to lincoln, nebraska?
9. dr. s. laura townsend started her practice at the harvard medical center.

Part III:
10. Rachel, kicker, PN
11. Rachel, ball, DO
12. She, best, PN
13. Rachel, award, DO
14. We, happy, PA

Part IV:
15. has
16. driven
17. Aren't
18. are, aren't

Unit II
Lesson 11
Part I:
1. simple
2. simple
3. compound; In 79 A.D. the mountain erupted violently, (and) the city of Pompeii was buried under 50 feet of ash and stone.
4. simple
5. simple
6. compound; Mount Saint Helens is near Vancouver, Washington, (and) it is part of the Cascade Mountains.
7. simple
8. simple
9. compound; The explosion blew 1,300 feet off the top of the volcano, (and) ash and rock flowed at 200 miles an hour down the mountain.
10. simple
11. simple
12. compound; Everything near the volcano was covered by up to 200 feet of ash, (and) ash blew east and south all the way across the United States.
13. compound; Mount Saint Helens's eruption was terrifying and destructive, (but) it was a small eruption compared to Mount Vesuvius.

Lessons 12 to 17

Lesson 12
Answers may vary.
1. There were wise people in ancient times, and they understood life, too.
2. Their statements were made long ago, but their wisdom is apparent today.
3. Cicero lived 2,000 years ago, and he was a famous Roman writer.
4. Cicero was an orator and a politician, but he is remembered for his writings.
5. He wrote about people's foolish ideas, and time has not proved him wrong.
6. People try to get ahead, and some do so at the expense of others.
7. Many things cannot be changed, but we worry about them anyway.
8. We want others to agree with us, but we are unwilling to change.
9. Do Cicero's words apply to us, or have we risen above foolish ideas?

Lesson 13
Answers will vary.
1. Augusta Rogers invented and patented the automobile heater.
2. Her invention did not use or cause fire.
3. Around 1770, William Addis broke British law and started a riot.
4. He and other people were put in prison.
5. Life in prison was very dull and very disagreeable.
6. Every day he washed his face and cleaned his teeth with a rag.
7. The ancients and everyone else had used rags to clean teeth.
8. William Addis invented the toothbrush and became an overnight success.

Lesson 14
Answers may vary
1. Arteries carry blood through the body, and veins also carry blood.
   Arteries and veins carry blood through the body.
2. The heart is like a machine, and it pumps blood constantly.
   The heart is like a machine and pumps blood constantly.
3. It pumps blood into the arteries, and it gets blood from the veins.
   It pumps blood into the arteries and gets blood from the veins.
4. Blood carries food to the body, and it carries oxygen to the body.
   Blood carries food and oxygen to the body.
5. We need oxygen constantly, and we can die from lack of "fuel."
   We need oxygen constantly and can die from lack of "fuel."
6. The heart, blood, and lungs never rest, but they work less during sleep.
   The heart, blood, and lungs never rest but work less during sleep.

Lesson 15
Part I:
1. Is the Fahrenheit scale the best way to tell temperature, or should we change?
2. Water freezes at 32° Fahrenheit, and it boils at 212° F.
3. Britain, the U.S., and other English-speaking countries often use this measure.
4. The rest of the world, however, uses the Celsius scale.
5. This scale, also called the centigrade scale, is easy to use.
6. On this simple scale water freezes at 0° C, and it boils at 100° C.
7. Are the freezing and boiling points of water separated by only 100 degrees?
8. Yes, they are, and this feature makes the scale easy to use.
9. How simple that must be!
10. Yes, it is simple, and it is used in scientific work.
11. The Celsius scale is used in science, engineering, and many other fields.
12. Old habits, of course, are hard to change.
13. Slowly, inch by inch, little by little, we are changing.
14. The change will affect our way of measuring temperature.
15. On February 10, 1964, our National Bureau of Standards started using the new system.

Part II: Answers will vary.
WORDSEARCH: continent

Lesson 16
Part I: Sentences will vary. The plural nouns should be spelled as shown.
1. flies   3. crashes   5. stories
2. women   4. pianos

Part II: Sentences will vary. The possessive forms should be spelled as shown.
6. JoAnne's   8. engines'   10. her, (hers)
7. our (ours)   9. brothers'

Lesson 17
Part I:
1. readers   2. Ms. Christie

3. customers
4. fiction
5. cases
6. minds, imaginations
7. publishers
8. Ms. Christie
9. world

Part II:
10. The Mysterious Affair at Style gives many exciting reading.
11. Agatha Christie's work gives her admirers pleasure.
12. Her travels provided these works some unusual settings.
13. All this has won Agatha Christie large audiences.

Lesson 18
The abbreviation following each underlined word should be written on the line.
1. desert, subj.; place, pred. noun
2. land, pred. noun
3. sunlight, subj.; sand, ind. obj.; rocks, ind. obj.; glow, dir. obj.
4. heat, subj.; glare, subj.; furnace, dir. obj.
5. rattlesnake, subj.; creature, pred. noun
6. thing, ind. obj.; feeling, dir. obj.
7. Sunset, subj.; traveler, ind. obj.; contrast, dir. obj.
8. Nightfall, subj.; landscape, dir. obj.

WORDSEARCH: paper

Lesson 19
The United States won its freedom from Great Britain, but the two nations were soon at war again. The fighting lasted more than two years, and the struggle became known as the War of 1812. The British, the Canadians, and their Indian allies won many battles. Fortunately, the Americans won some victories. On January 8, 1815, a major battle was fought at New Orleans, Louisiana. British troops, led by General Sir Edward Packenham, attacked smaller American forces, led by General Andrew Jackson. The British attacked in closed ranks. The Americans stayed hidden. The order to Jackson's troops was, "Don't fire till you see the whites of their eyes!" Over two thousand British troops were killed, but only 13 Americans died. The battle, however, came *after* the treaty was signed.
COMPOSITION: Answers will vary.

Lesson 20
Part I:
1. sidewalk's
2. pitchers'
3. women's
4. sheep's

Parts II–VII: Answers will vary.

Unit III
Lesson 21
Part I:
(At the age) (of ten) I became interested (in cars). We had an old car (on blocks) (in the backyard). My parents let me work (on it). I would rise (at seven) (in the morning) and play (with the valves and carburetor). (By age sixteen) I had rebuilt engines (from a dozen cars). I took a job (in a garage) and worked (on weekends) and (during the summer). I saved $250 (in six months) and bought a sedan (with a cracked engine block). (At the end) (of a year) (of hard work), it was ready. I towed it (from my backyard) (to a local strip) and entered the time trials. That car had a terrible time (in the quarter mile), but I got quite a thrill (from my ride) (down the dusty strip). It was a start, and someday, (with luck), I'll break the land speed record (at Bonneville)!
Part II: Answers will vary.
WORDSEARCH: China

Lesson 22
Part I: The following words should be underlined:
1. Jim, book, week
2. Greg, Anne, Jim, books, time
3. Jim, book, purpose
4. book, memory
5. Brent, lunchbox, Jim, stairs
6. Brent, sandwiches, lunchbox, Jim
7. time, Jim, Lorre, concert
8. Jim, Lorre, house, taxi
9. librarians, Jim, dollars, book
10. expense, memory

Part II: The following words should be underlined:
11. He; it
12. They; he; them
13. he; it
14. It
15. He; it
16. He; them; he; it; him
17. he; her
18. he; she
19. They; him; it
20. it

Lesson 23
Part I:
1. We 2. Our 3. We, they 4. They, us

Part II:
5. herself
6. yourself
7. themselves
8. myself
9. ourselves

Part III:
10. Who 11. Which 12. Whose 13. What
14. Whom

Part IV:
15. herself, compound personal
16. us, personal
17. Who, interrogative
18. Which, interrogative
19. You, personal
20. himself, compound personal
21. What, interrogative
22. she, personal

Lessons 24 to 33

Lesson 24
Part I:
1. These 2. this 3. those 4. that

Part II:
5. Anyone 7. all 9. None
6. someone 8. some

Part III:
10. yours, mine 12. Ours 14. mine
11. his 13. her

Part IV:
15. that, demonstrative
16. his, possessive
17. all, indefinite
18. these, demonstrative
19. her, possessive

Lesson 25
1. subj.
2. dir. obj.
3. subj.
4. obj. of prep.
5. subj.
6. obj. of prep.
7. ind. obj.
8. obj. of prep.
9. subj.
10. dir. obj.
11. dir. obj.
12. ind. obj.
13. pred. nom.
14. obj. of prep.
15. subj.
16. obj. of prep.
17. subj.
18. dir. obj.
19. obj. of prep.
20. ind. obj.

Lesson 26
Part I:
1. their; nurses
2. she; doctor
3. his, her; doctor
4. their; Art, Marie
5. her; Greta
6. their; Aides
7. her; Dr. Adams
8. their; doctors
9. he, she; doctor
10. their; doctors

Part II:
11. his
12. his
13. her
14. his, her
15. their
16. their
17. their
18. his
19. his
20. his

Lesson 27
Answers will vary.

Lesson 28
1. no 5. no 9. yes 13. no 17. yes
2. no 6. yes 10. yes 14. no
3. yes 7. no 11. no 15. yes
4. no 8. no 12. no 16. no

WORDSEARCH: skin diving

Lesson 29
Part I:
1. known 3. between 5. Whose
2. Those 4. Its 6. theirs
7. gone 11. into 15. saw
8. Between 12. written 16. seen
9. taken 13. taken 17. seen
10. from 14. done

Part II: Answers will vary.
COMPOSITION: Answers will vary.

Lesson 30
Parts I and II: Answers will vary.

Unit IV
Lesson 31
The word after each underlined word should be written on the line.
1. This, leader; fiery, leader; brilliant, leader; first, container; effective, container; fresh, food
2. large, sum; first, prize; special, contest
3. new, way; fresh, food
4. Every, inventor; clever, inventor; French, inventor; that, prize; fat, prize
5. many, years; this, problem; difficult, problem
6. fresh, foods; sturdy, bottles; glass, bottles
7. warm, bottles; steamy, bottles; cork, stoppers
8. full, bottles; large, pot; hot, water
9. This, method; simple, method; effective, method; harmful, bacteria
10. this, Parisian; bright, Parisian; patient, Parisian; rich, prize

Lesson 32
1. numerous reptiles
2. smaller numbers
3. existent tortoises
4. isolated Galápagos Islands
5. difficult survival
6. aware sailors
7. weary, bored, hungry sailors
8. perfect stop
9. delicious meat
10. slow animals
11. healthy tortoises
12. incredible cruelty
13. scarce tortoises
14. long, sad story
15. possible extinction

Lesson 33
Answers may vary.
1. Its tiny mint mark is below the wreath.
2. Charlotte, North Carolina, once had a small United States mint.
3. Did the mint produce small quantities of gold coins?
4. Its valuable coins are prized by collectors.

Lessons 33 to 39

5. Was the dusty attic filled with old boxes?
6. I found a worn coin purse there.
7. It held an elegant 1853-c one-dollar gold piece!

WORDSEARCH: snake

Lesson 34
1. is officially ruled
2. has ruled quietly
3. live simply
4. long ago abolished
5. are productively employed
6. live happily
7. is approximately
8. primarily speak
9. is probably best known
10. is limited mainly
11. warmly welcomes
12. do not vote
13. may change soon

Part II: Answers will vary.

Lesson 35
Part I:
1. more; expensive; adj.
2. incredibly; loud; adj.
3. almost; everywhere; adv.
4. just; barely; adv.
5. extremely; large; adj.
6. very; proudly; adv.
7. certainly; noticeable; adj.
8. completely; transparent; adj.
9. somewhat; similar; adj.
10. nearly; three; adj.
11. incredibly; fast; adv.
12. not; quite; adv.

Part II: Answers will vary.

Lesson 36
Part I:
1. of the detective; hair
2. for this odd disguise; reason
3. of the Silver Scream Waxworks; owner
4. of his wax figures; faces
5. of the detective; task
6. of this mad torcher; capture
7. in the building; guard
8. beside a wax Humphrey Bogart; pedestal

Part II:
9. above the wax Elizabeth I; appeared
10. down the aisle; was creeping
11. toward the detective's face; raised
12. From the pedestal; leaped
13. with an iron grip; grabbed
14. by the torcher's face; was shocked

15. To her surprise; had caught
16. in her life; had had

Lesson 37
Part I:
1. after the Civil War (was invented); adverb
2. (invention) of Christopher Sholes; adjective
3. (editor) for a Wisconsin newspaper; adjective
4. (patent) on the typewriter; adjective
5. Through the years (have been improved); adverb
6. (depend) on them; adverb
7. (could operate) without one; adverb
8. (Writers) of every kind; adjective
9. (have switched) to word processors; adverb
10. (keys) of Sholes's typewriter; adjective
11. (surprise) to the inventor; adjective

Part II: Answers will vary.

Lesson 38
Correct words are in italics. (Corrections of double negatives may vary.)

Neither of them has *any* experience. But *they're ready to* learn. Sergei *heard* about a training program last week. He signed up as *quickly* as he could. He *may* become a forklift operator. *It's* not easy to *raise* pallets without upsetting them. But Sergei *doesn't* worry *about* learning. And he *hasn't ever* been a quitter. Elnora *may* have a job in a tire warehouse. If you *were* to ask her, she would tell you *proudly* of her skills. If she can't be *taught* to be a supervisor, nobody *can*. Elnora's not afraid of *hard* work, either. *Her* arms and legs *are* strong from exercising *regularly*. She never *sits* down when *there's* work to do. My friends hope to begin work *immediately*. They may not be *successful* this week, but *they're sure* to be hired in the near future.

WORDSEARCH: coal

Lesson 39
In the southwestern town of Okemah, Oklahoma, Woody Guthrie was born in 1912. He was a poor boy with itchy feet and great talents. During his youth he rode freight trains all over the United States. His uncle had taught him to play the guitar, and his guitar was always with him. He composed songs about penniless travelers, about ordinary people, and even about the Bonneville Dam. He truly traveled from New York to California. He wrote a book about himself, too, called Bound for Glory. He was just becoming famous when he became very ill. He spent the last fifteen years of his life in a hospital. However, people today sing his songs more than ever. Hasn't everyone heard his song "This Land Is Your Land"? The Okemah Library, in his hometown, has paid him

Lessons 39 to 45

a tribute. His music is recorded in the Library of Congress. A power plant in the Pacific Northwest was named in his honor. Woody Guthrie will be remembered by the country he loved.
COMPOSITION: Answers will vary.

Lesson 40
Part I:
1. Ronald Reagan was inaugurated president on Jan. 20, 1981, in Washington, D.C.
2. This event was celebrated with a parade, formal dinners, balls, and speeches.
3. Of course, many people attended the festivities.
4. Jon, did you get to go?
5. No, but it must have been exciting!

Part II:
6. Casey did all of his work on Tuesday.
7. The Greensboro High School band marched in the parade last week.
8. Mrs. Jenner hasn't taught me anything.
9. Zac and Jerry were lying down when they should have gone to work.
10. I saw you when you were racing at Daytona.

Part III:
11. slowly, calmly, angry
12. dark, silent, deadly
13. completely, incompetent, Maria's, so, unevenly, flat
14. thoroughly, wire

Part IV:
15. in the trunk
16. to the kitchen, of milk
17. between two pages, of a heavy book
18. Among the stars, of the brightest
19. into the house, of flowers
20. of shoes, with rubber soles

Unit V
Lesson 41
Part I:
1. beginning
2. using
3. taking
4. flying
5. lying
6. seeing
7. driving
8. forgetting
9. paying
10. stopping

Part II:
11. planned
12. carried
13. said
14. saved
15. caught
16. matched
17. filled
18. tied
19. made
20. took

Part III: Answers will vary.
WORDSEARCH: bee

Lesson 42
Part I: The following words should *not* be marked through:
1. goes
2. reads
3. are
4. has
5. meets
6. is
7. gets
8. speaks
9. sell
10. pay
11. try
12. agree

Part II: Answers will vary.

Lesson 43
Part I: The following words should *not* be marked through:
1. is
2. speaks
3. listens
4. tell
5. gives
6. reflects
7. reveal
8. was
9. knows
10. think
11. is
12. find
13. have
14. stare
15. grasps

Part II: Answers will vary.

Lesson 44
1. teaches; present
2. will have; future
3. is using; present
4. taught; past
5. was teaching; past
6. want; present
7. makes; present
8. uses; present
9. was; past
10. left; past
11. imported; past
12. Will be; future

Part II: Sentences will vary. The past forms of the verbs are shown.
13. did   14. drew   15. drank

Lesson 45
Part I: Corrected verbs are in italics.

Before 1908 inventors and airplane builders did their own flying. These *were* careful and patient people who safely *tested* their own planes and *had* long careers. After 1908 the birdmen and birdwomen appeared. Daring and reckless, they *flew* for excitement and prize money at air shows. They flew stunts and tested planes, and many of them *died* in crashes. Each crash *caused* the builder to improve that plane.

Lincoln Beachey *had* a successful career as a show balloonist before he *began* flying at 17. In 1906 he *became* famous when he *made* the first flight around the Washington Monument. He flew under bridges and over Niagara Falls, and he *scooped* handkerchiefs off the ground with his wing tip. Always a show-off, he *dressed* up to fly against Blanche Stuart Scott, a rival flier. He barely avoided a crash, flew loops, and *thrilled* the crowd. He *drowned* in San Francisco Bay in 1915 when the monoplane he had designed *folded* in the air during the World's Fair. The Birdman Era *ended* with his death.

Part II: Answers will vary.
WORDSEARCH: petroleum

Lesson 46
Part I:
1. developed, active
2. was developed, passive
3. named, active
4. was named, passive
5. was introduced, passive
6. introduced, active
7. introduced, active
8. was introduced, passive
9. was produced, passive
10. did produce, active

Part II: Answers may vary.
11. A photograph can give pleasure.
12. A camera shows views of the world.

Lesson 47
Part I:
1. we'll
2. it's
3. won't
4. doesn't
5. haven't
6. they're
7. you're
8. we've
9. who's
10. hasn't

Part II: Answers will vary.
11. can't
12. don't, it's
13. doesn't
14. She's
15. hasn't
16. don't (or: won't)
17. can't
18. Aren't

Part III: Answers will vary.

Lesson 48:
Part I:
1. is
2. appears
3. costs
4. comes
5. issued
6. had
7. decided
8. known
9. is
10. issued
11. guaranteed
12. coined
13. supervises
14. are
15. wears
16. last

Part II: Answers will vary.

Lesson 49
Part I:
1. Jamaica is one of the islands in the Caribbean Sea.
2. Kingston, Jamaica, has almost the same temperature summer and winter.
3. The Blue Mountains are in the eastern part, and heavy rain falls there.
4. The hurricane season, August to November, brings damaging storms.
5. Christopher Columbus landed on the island of Jamaica in 1494.
6. The Arawak Indians lived there then, but Spanish settlers killed most of them.
7. The Spanish brought in African slaves to work on plantations.
8. Many Europeans, Chinese, and East Indians later settled in Jamaica.
9. The island became a British colony in 1670.
10. On August 6, 1962, Jamiaica gained its independence.
11. A Jamaican artist, Namba Roy, became well known in Great Britain.
12. Another islander, Claude McKay, came to the United States.
13. He wrote such books as Harlem Shadows and Banana Bottom.

Part II: Answers will vary.
COMPOSITION: Answers will vary.

Lesson 50
Part I:
1. are
2. Is
3. do
4. were
5. are

Part II:
6. broke
7. forgot
8. threw
9. carried
10. stopped
11. took
12. found
13. laid
14. sat
15. wrote

Part III:
16. it's
17. she'll
18. didn't
19. wouldn't
20. won't
21. they're
22. I'm
23. Casey's
24. hasn't
25. don't
26. you'll
27. haven't

Unit VI
Lesson 51
Part I:
1. borrowed car
2. fallen tree
3. rented truck
4. dented fender
5. unplanned delay
6. prepared dinner
7. torn curtains
8. brewed coffee
9. rolling hills
10. congested traffic
11. rumpled, wrinkled clothes

Part II:
12. radio (sitting on the table)
13. parts (taken from other radios)
14. tools (borrowed from her friend)
15. Wires (soldered together)
16. plans (bought at a hardware store)
17. Parts (ordered from the East Coast)

Lessons 51 to 64

18. <u>programs</u> (broadcast from Canada)
19. <u>job</u> (repairing small appliances)
20. <u>person</u> (offering office space)
21. <u>appliances</u> (repaired by a skilled worker)

Lesson 52
Part I: Answers may vary.
1. Waiting for a bus, Tony and his boss witnessed the accident.
2. The truck, taking the turn too fast, ran into a parked car.
3. The car, dented in two places, would probably still run.
4. Police officers arriving at the scene took Tony's statement.

Part II: Answers may vary.
5. Walking to the store, I saw a new office building.
6. Jane gave a book written by Aileen Fisher to her niece.
7. Paying his check, he hurried out the door.
8. I gave a roast turkey wrapped in aluminum foil to my sister.

Lesson 53
Part I:
1. Tumbling; subj.
2. packing; dir. obj.
3. Waiting; subj.
4. Worrying; subj.
5. discussing; dir. obj.
6. Snorkeling; subj.
7. snapping; subj. comp.
8. teaching; subj. comp.

Part II: Answers will vary.

Lesson 54
Part I:
1. (Finding new space travelers) is
2. does mind (spending long days on the road)
3. (Telling women and members of minority groups about the space shuttle) is
4. (Talking with Ms. Nichols) has interested
5. Would enjoy (piloting a ship through space)
6. (Recruiting for NASA) has pleased
7. believes (encouraging people toward a space career)

Part II: Answers will vary.

Lesson 55
Part I:
1. To search   3. To dig up   5. To find
2. to find   4. to recover

Part II:
6. to hunt   8. to be found 10. to verify
7. to search   9. to fight

Part III:
11. to look   13. to outrun   15. to fall
12. to know   14. to call

WORDSEARCH: building

Unit VII
Lesson 61
Part I:
1. Because   6. Although
2. whenever   7. Since
3. because   8. because
4. Although   9. When
5. where   10. if

Part II:
11. (If we understood sharks better)
12. (While sharks are killers)
13. (Although the whale shark is huge)
14. (unless they are aroused)
15. (if it meets a healthy creature its own size)
16. (While a shark looks big to us)
17. (since they often attack people)
18. (that people must avoid)
19. (If we consider size and viciousness)
20. (Although most sharks live in salt water)

Lesson 62
Answers may vary.
1. Although some were powerful, others had no influence on their governments.
2. Because they are elected to important positions, women have more power in government today.
3. When Indira Gandhi was elected prime minister of India in 1966, she became the first woman ever elected to head a major government.
4. Although Mrs. Gandhi was defeated in 1977, she was reelected in 1980.
5. When Israeli Prime Minister Levi Eshkol died in 1969, Golda Meir was appointed to take his place and served until 1974.
6. After the Conservatives won control of the House of Commons in 1979, Margaret Thatcher became Britain's first female prime minister.
7. As women such as these gain experience and respect, more women will be elected to influential positions.

Lesson 63
Answers will vary.

Lesson 64
Part I:
1. people (who want better vocabularies)

Lessons 64 to 68

2. Greek, Latin (which are two ancient languages)
3. reason (why *territory* means "an area of land")
4. word (that means "land" or "earth")
5. times (when you meet similar words)
6. words (that come from the same root)
7. meaning (that these three words share)
8. age (when people are exploring space)
9. person (whose job is the exploration of space)
10. terms (that mean "star" and "sailor")

Part II: Answers may vary.
11. which
12. that (or which)
13. which
14. who
15. that (or which)
16. that (or which)
17. who
18. that (or which)
19. that (or which)
20. who

Lesson 65
Part I:
1. Although I had visited South America, I had never been to Mexico.
2. While we were flying over Texas, we passed through a storm.
3. After our plane landed in Mexico City, we checked into our hotel.
4. When we finished unpacking, we took a long walk.
5. We were often short of breath because the city is at a high altitude.
6. Since Mexico City has many fine restaurants, we dined very well.
7. After we had lunch, we took a short nap.
8. After a short drive through the city, we headed for Taxco and Acapulco.
9. As we drove, a huge snowcapped volcano came into view.
10. We were quite awed when we saw Popocatepetl, the famous peak.
11. Although it was close, it seemed faraway.
12. We could see the peak clearly because the day was so bright and sunny.
13. We followed the main road until we reached the Taxco turnoff.
14. After we spent a week enjoying Mexico City's activity, Taxco was a pleasant change.
15. We spent several hours on the beach at Acapulco because the weather was so beautiful.
16. When you spend a week in Acapulco, you return home with a better outlook on life.

Part II: Answers will vary.

Lesson 66
Answers may vary.
1. Anne studied literature at a community college, and she worked for a publisher.
   After Anne studied literature at a community college, she worked for a publisher.
2. She was still in school but two of her stories were published.
   While she was still in school, two of her stories were published.
3. Anne graduated with honors, and she wrote for magazines.
   After Anne graduated with honors, she wrote for magazines.
4. She sold many fine stories, but her first story was rejected.
   Although her first story was rejected, she sold many fine stories.
5. She worked hard, and her stories were successful.
   Her stories were successful because she worked very hard.
6. Anne wrote a very fine story, and she expanded it into a novel.
   After Anne wrote a very fine story, she expanded it into a novel.

Lesson 67
Answers will vary.
WORDSEARCH: wasp

Lesson 68
Corrected words are in italics.

Scott Joplin was one of the *great* musicians and composers in our *history*. When he was *fourteen* years old, he headed *for* Missouri. He *played* the piano *there* and on *riverboats*. He was good at playing a new kind of music. This music had a *funny* and *tricky beat*, so it was *called* "ragged time" music, or "ragtime." *Later*, his *friends* urged him to *study* music. He *became* a composer *using* the style of ragtime music to *write everything* from ballets to operas. His *popular* music, *called* "rags," was *very well* known. The "Maple Leaf Rag" is *especially famous*. However, no *one* was *interested* in Joplin's *serious* music. *People would listen* to him play but were not willing to *give* him credit as a *writer* of serious music. He *continued* to work hard, *though* his operas *failed*. His most *ambitious* work was the opera "Treemonisha." He put all his *money* into a *performance* of it. It was a *disaster* that *destroyed* him. He *died* in a hospital in 1917. He is considered a *unique* composer, and he is *loved* and *admired throughout* the world.

WORDSEARCH: eye

Lessons 56 to 76

Lesson 56
Part I:
1. (to throw a party)
2. (to show a video replay of the match)
3. (to swim)
4. (to ask the tennis pro some questions)
5. (to play a drop shot)
6. (to practice more)
7. (To win a tournament)
8. (to bring their trophies)

Part II: Answers will vary.

Lesson 57
Part I:
1. wide
2. empty
3. hurt
4. watchful
5. slim
6. keep
7. warning
8. rules
9. bones

Part II:
10. sad
11. close
12. quiet
13. worst
14. superior
15. bright
16. lower
17. smooth
18. well

WORDSEARCH: metric

Lesson 58
Part I:
1. carries
2. tells
3. looks
4. needs
5. thinks
6. seems
7. says
8. sees
9. sells
10. save
11. charges
12. begin
13. signs
14. hears

Part II: Answers will vary.

Lesson 59
Answers will vary.

Lesson 60
Parts I–IV: Answers will vary.

Lesson 69
Answers will vary.

Lesson 70
Answers will vary.

Unit VIII
Lesson 71

109 Hales Drive
Springfield, Missouri 65811
February 16, 1983

Product Manager for Batteries
Speedy Flash Products, Inc.
725 Princeton Ave.
Des Moines, Iowa 50309

Dear Product Manager:

    Two months ago I put three Speedy Flash batteries into my flashlight. These batteries have corroded and cannot be removed. Since you guarantee to replace any flashlight damaged by your batteries, I am sending my flashlight to you for replacement.

                      Yours truly,
                      Dana Hobbie

WORDSEARCH: France

Lesson 72
Answers will vary.

Lesson 73
Answers will vary.

Lesson 74
Answers will vary.

Lesson 75
1. thought; length
2. (b)
3. Robins are *birds* that live in both the *city* and the country. In the city, *cats* may attack robins. In the *country*, robins may have other enemies. Cats move much faster than *dogs*. Perhaps that is why dogs *don't* worry birds very much.
4. (a) false
   (b) true
   (c) true
5. (b)

Lesson 76
1. compound
2. subjective complements
3. main; dependent
4. past
5. dependent
6. me; you; him; her; it; us; them (any three)
7. verb; adjective
8. imperative

Lessons 76 to 81

9. subject; verb
10. verb; subject
11. object
12. -ing
13. antecedent
14. sentence
15. dependent clause
16. adjective; adverb
17. prepositions

Lesson 77
Answers will vary.
WORDSEARCH: invention

Lesson 78
Part I: Appropriate forms are in italics.

It was summer in the tropics. Six fat clouds *lay* lazily about the baby blue sky. Two figures in white *sat* in the shade of a tattered green awning. Before them *lay* a jetsam-covered beach and the blue Pacific.

"Then, are we all *set* for tomorrow morning?" asked the shell collector. He slowly and dramatically *laid* his open hand on the table top.

"It's all been *laid* out as you asked," said the trader, showing no emotion. "The boat arrangements are now *set*. The diver is *sitting* in the hotel waiting for instructions. Tomorrow afternoon you should be *sitting* aboard the flight to Auckland. And the treasure should be *lying* safely in your flight bag."

"Good," said the collector. Five $1000 bills were *laid* on the table. There would be five more for the trader if all went as planned. The treasure at that moment *lay* somewhere out in the Pacific. It was calmly poisoning its dinner. The collector had *set* his mind on coming away with the largest specimen of Glory-of-the-Seas ever sighted. Nowadays only a few of these cones *lie* on the ocean floor. Prized by collectors, these creatures have shells of overwhelming beauty.

But the biggest mistake one can make is to greedily pick up a Glory-of-the-Seas *lying* on the sandy bottom. It will send its tiny harpoon into your skin. You'll *sit* down. Then you'll *lie* down. And you'll probably never get up.

Not all the danger *lies* in the catching of this deadly beauty. The collector knew this only too well. He *lay* awake all night on the hammock, thinking through the plan again and again and again.
Part II: Answers will vary.

Lesson 79
1. accept	ac-cept
2. application	ap-pli-ca-tion
3. appointment	ap-point-ment
4. dependable	de-pend-able
5. deposit	de-pos-it
6. driving	driv-ing
7. envelope	en-ve-lope
8. garage	ga-rage
9. hundred	hun-dred
10. invoice	in-voice
11. niece	niece
12. order	or-der
13. quiet	qui-et
14. rather	rath-er
15. razor	ra-zor
16. really	re-al-ly
17. stopper	stop-per
18. thought	thought

COMPOSITION: Answers will vary.

Lesson 80
Answers will vary.

Unit IX
Lesson 81
Part I:
1. The great whales and dolphins are mammals. *simple*
2. They breathe air, and the females nurse their young with milk. *compound*
3. When they want to breathe, they must go to the surface. *complex*
4. The blue whale is the world's biggest animal. *simple*
5. Dolphins and porpoises look similar, but they are different. *compound*
6. The dolphin's greater size and intelligence set it apart. *simple*
7. Cetaceans often swim together and communicate with each other. *simple*
8. When a dolphin gets sick, another dolphin helps it. *complex*
9. The sick dolphin rests, and the "nurse" helps it to the surface. *compound*
10. Female cetaceans often help another female when a calf is born. *complex*
11. Many dolphins and whales have large and complex brains. *simple*
12. Scientists are studying dolphin communication. *simple*

Part II: Answers will vary.

Lessons 82 to 88

Lesson 82

1. Rain | fell
2. Luis | likes | music
3. birds | ate | seeds
   - blue
   - small
   - Four
4. Grasshoppers | eat | leaves
   - green
5. brother | won | contest
   - My
   - first
   - the

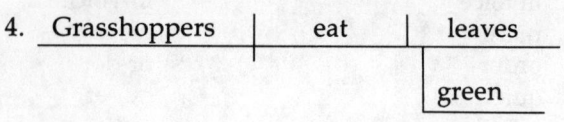

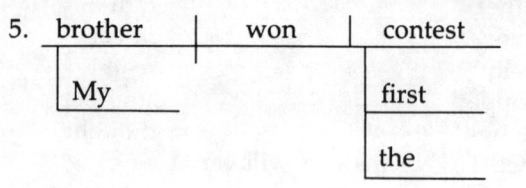

Lesson 83

1. to play the trumpet, infinitive
2. marching, participle
3. Playing trumpet, gerund
4. music-reading, participle
5. to marry Lillian Hardin, infinitive
6. recording, participle
7. trumpeting, gerund
8. Visiting many countries, gerund
9. to introduce American jazz to Europeans, infinitive
10. featured, participle
11. entertaining, gerund
12. playing, gerund

Parts II–IV: Answers will vary.

Lesson 84

Part I:
1. that reportedly has a monster; adjective
2. Because people love monster tales; adverb
3. who are fascinated by the legend; adjective
4. which is very deep; adjective
5. When clear pictures are finally taken; adverb

Part II: Answers may vary.
6. Some people believe in the monster because they are fascinated by strange things.
7. Since I've never seen a clear picture of it, I don't believe in the monster.
8. While I was in Scotland, I stopped at Loch Ness to look for the monster.
9. Until I saw the thick fog, I didn't realize the foolishness of my plan.

WORDSEARCH: glass

Lesson 85

Part I: The following words should *not* be marked through.

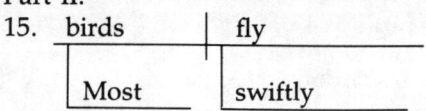

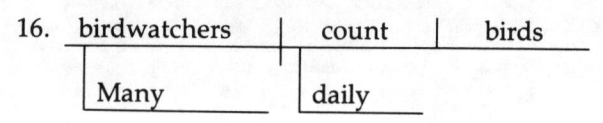

1. show
2. lay
3. represent
4. grows
5. fall
6. is
7. have
8. are
9. is
10. beats
11. provide
12. list
13. identify
14. does

Part II:
15. birds | fly
    - Most
    - swiftly
16. birdwatchers | count | birds
    - Many
    - daily

Lesson 86

Part I: Answers will vary.

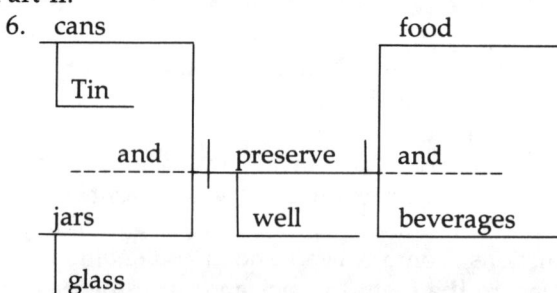

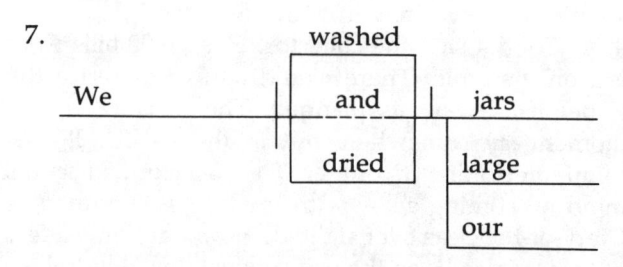

Part II:
6. cans | food
   - Tin
   - and | preserve | and
   - jars | well | beverages
   - glass
7. We | washed and dried | jars
   - large
   - our

Lesson 87

Answers will vary.

Lesson 88

1. doesn't
2. very
3. any
4. took
5. did
6. saw
7. those
8. sat
9. teach
10. you're
11. into
12. its
13. well
14. given
15. her
16. ever
17. one
18. it's

WORDSEARCH: book

Lesson 89

916 North Aspen Street
Cumberland, Indiana 46229
July 19, 1985

Mrs. Alice Webb
Webb and Skogsted Insurance Brokers
100 Sunrise Boulevard
Fort Wayne, Indiana 46800

Dear Mrs. Webb:

On June 6, 1985, I wrote you asking how to purchase medical insurance. You sent me a pamphlet entitled "Protection and Peace of Mind." You also wrote that you would call me soon to arrange a meeting. I have heard nothing since then, and I have been unable to reach you by phone. If I don't hear from you by Thursday, July 24, I will go elsewhere for my insurance.

Sincerely,
Felipe Alvarez

COMPOSITION: Answers will vary.

Lesson 90

Part I:
1. set, lay
2. gone
3. there
4. Who's
5. frozen
6. among
7. There
8. teach
9. are
10. us

Answers will vary on questions 11 and 12.

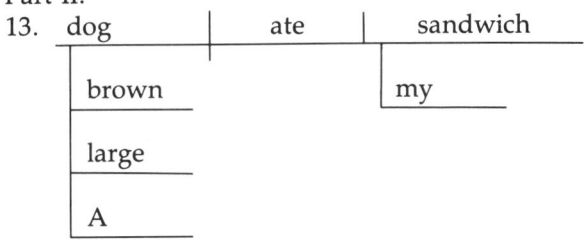

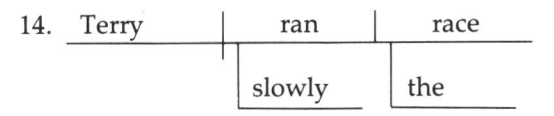

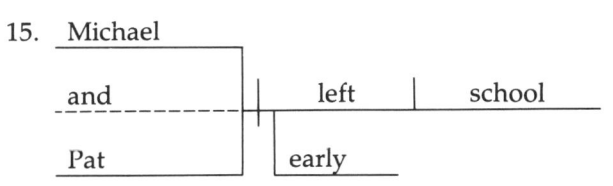

Part II:
13. dog / ate / sandwich; brown, large, A (under dog); my (under sandwich)
14. Terry / ran / race; slowly, the
15. Michael and Pat / left / school; early

Part III:
16. to play, infinitive
17. printed, participle
18. to save, infinitive
19. to begin, infinitive
20. Decaying, participle
21. hunting, fishing, gerund, gerund
22. to go, infinitive

Answers will vary on questions 23–25.

Part IV:
26. (under) the bed, (in) the middle bedroom
27. (with) plastic wrap, (on) the table
28. (between) aisles eight and nine, (on) a display rack
29. (for) Miami, (near) the first, (of) July

Part V:
30. I (S), them (OP)
31. She (S), him (IO)
32. us (IO)
33. He (S), it (DO)
34. They (S), her (OP)

Part VI:
35. complex, while you check out
36. simple
37. compound, (and)
38. complex, After we finish here
39. simple
40. complex, Since we forgot her birthday last year
41. compound, (but)
42. complex, After we eat dinner
43. simple
44. simple

Part VII:

it's hard to imagine a time without stereos, hamburgers, zippers, and paper cups, but there's a first time for everything. did you know that leonardo da vinci designed the first contact lenses in 1508? these lenses were to fit over the white part of the eye. the first lenses were not made, however, until 1887, and they were quite uncomfortable. if you had lived in the seventeenth century and were hard of hearing, you could have used an ear trumpet. the ear trumpet was a long horn. you put the small end in your ear and the large end toward the sound. alexander graham bell invented the first electronic hearing aid in 1876. the chinese used ice cellars more than three thousand years ago, but it wasn't until late in the nineteenth century that we had our first home refrigerator. the modern safety razor with a disposable blade was first sold by k. c. gillette in 1903, and col. jacob schick patented the first electric shaver in 1923.

INDEX TO GUIDES

(The numbers refer to guide numbers, not page numbers.)

Abbreviations: *see*
   Capitalization, Punctuation
Adjectives: *see* Parts of speech
Adverbs: *see* Parts of speech
Antonyms: *see* Dictionary
Apostrophe: *see* Punctuation
Application forms: 58
Appositives: 53
Articles: *see* Parts of speech
Capitalization
   Abbreviations: 42, 44
   Addresses: 43
   Beginning of sentence: 39a
   Days of week: 39d
   Envelopes: 56
   Holidays: 39f
   I: 39g
   Initials: 40
   Letters: 55
   Months: 39e
   Proper adjectives: 39c
   Proper nouns: 39b
   Quotations: 47
   Titles: 46
   Titles of respect: 41
Commas: *see* Punctuation
Conjunctions: *see* Parts of speech
Contractions: 29
Dictionary
   Alphabetical order: 57b
   Antonyms: 57d
   Synonyms: 57d
   Uses: 57a
   Word division: 57c
Double negatives: 35
Initials: *see* Capitalization, Punctuation
Letters
   Business: 55
   Envelopes: 56
Lie, lay: 32
Nouns: *see* Parts of speech
Oral exercises
   Wordsearch: 59
Paragraphs: 54
Parts of speech
   Adjectives: 33
      Articles: 33b
      Demonstrative: 33c
      Possessive nouns and pronouns: 33d

      Predicate adjectives: 8
      Proper adjectives: 33f
      Verbs: 33e
   Adverbs: 34
      Modifying adjectives: 34b
      Modifying adverbs: 34c
   Conjunctions: 37
      Compound elements: 37a, c
      Compound sentences: 37b
   Interjections: 38
   Nouns: 12–14
      Common: 12
      Plural: 13
      Possessive: 14
   Prepositions: 36
      As adjectives: 36c
      As adverbs: 36d
   Pronouns: 16–21
      Compound personal: 16
      Contractions: 29
      Demonstrative: 18
      Indefinite: 19
      Interrogative: 17
      Personal: 15a, b
      Possessive: 20
      Relative: 21
      Sentence elements: 15
   Verbs: 22–27
      Active: 24a
      Agreement with subject: 25
      Contractions: 29
      Gerunds: 28c, d
      Infinitives: 28e, f
      Intransitive: 22, 23a
      Linking: 22, 23c
      Participles: 28a, b
      Passive: 24b
      Phrases: 22
      Present participle: 26
      Principal parts: 26
      Tense forms: 27
      Transitive: 22, 23a
Periods: *see* Punctuation
Prepositions: *see* Parts of speech
Pronouns: *see* Parts of speech
Punctuation
   Apostrophe
      Contractions: 29
      Possessives: 14

   Commas
      Addresses: 43–45
      After *yes* and *no:* 50
      Appositives: 53
      Dates: 48
      Direct address: 49
      Direct quotations: 47
      Interrupting words: 51
      Series: 52
   Exclamation points: 2d
   Periods
      Abbreviations: 40–42
      Addresses: 43–45
      Declarative sentences: 2a
      Direct quotations: 47
      Imperative sentences: 2c
      Initials: 40
   Question marks: 2b
   Quotation marks: 46, 47
Sentences
   Complete: 1
   Complex: 11
   Compound: 10
   Declarative: 2a
   Dependent clauses: 11
   Direct objects: 6
   Exclamatory: 2d
   Imperative: 2c
   Indirect object: 7
   Interrogative: 2b
   Natural order: 3
   Simple: 9
   Subjective complement: 8
   Subjects: 4
   Verbs: 5
Sit, set: 31
Synonyms: *see* Dictionary
Titles: *see* Capitalization, Punctuation
Titles of respect: *see* Capitalization, Punctuation
Verbs: *see* Parts of speech
Wordsearch: 59